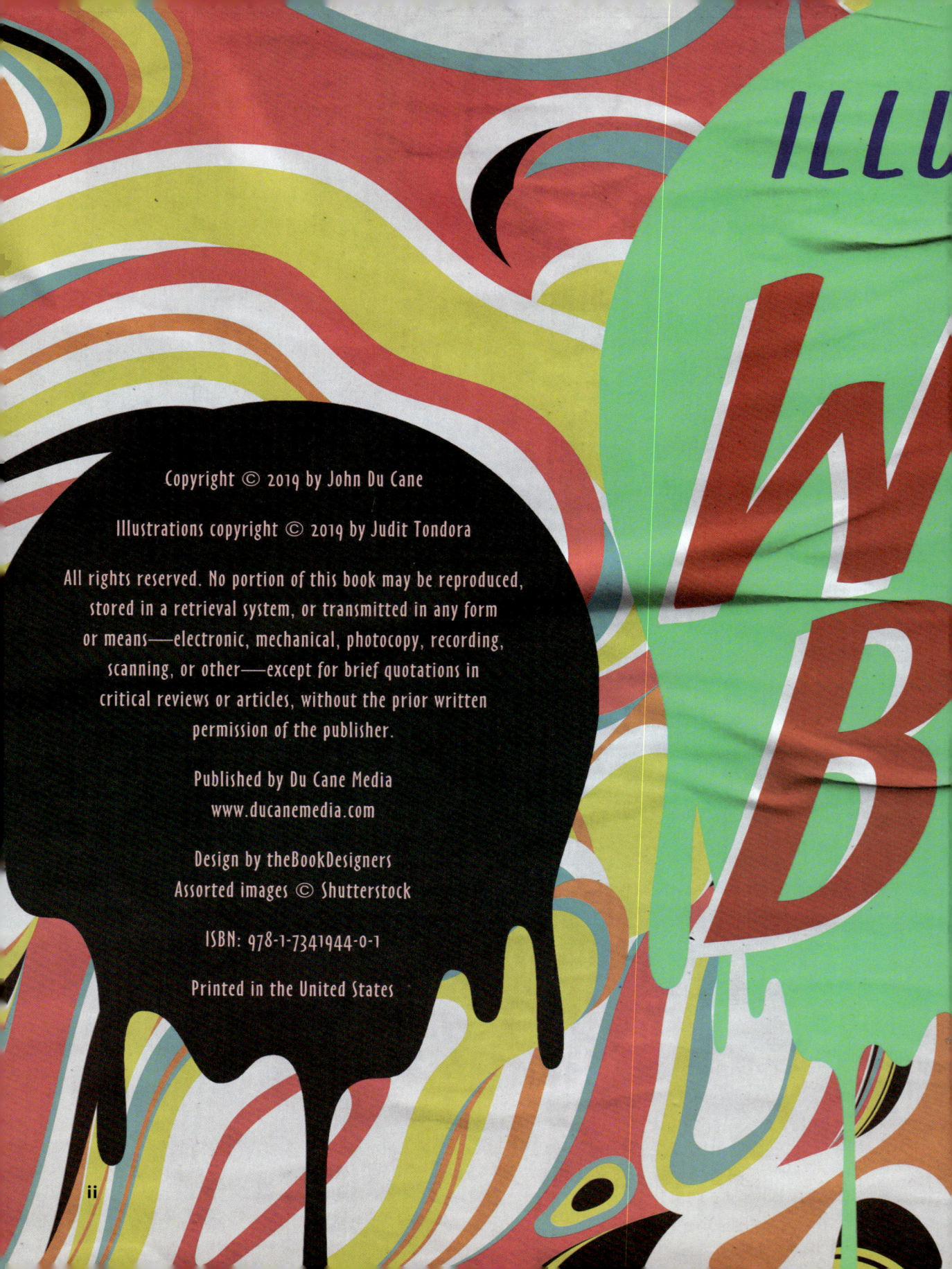

Published by Du Cane Media
www.ducanemedia.com

Design by theBookDesigners
Assorted images © Shutterstock

ISBN: 978-1-7341944-0-1

Printed in the United States

CONTENTS

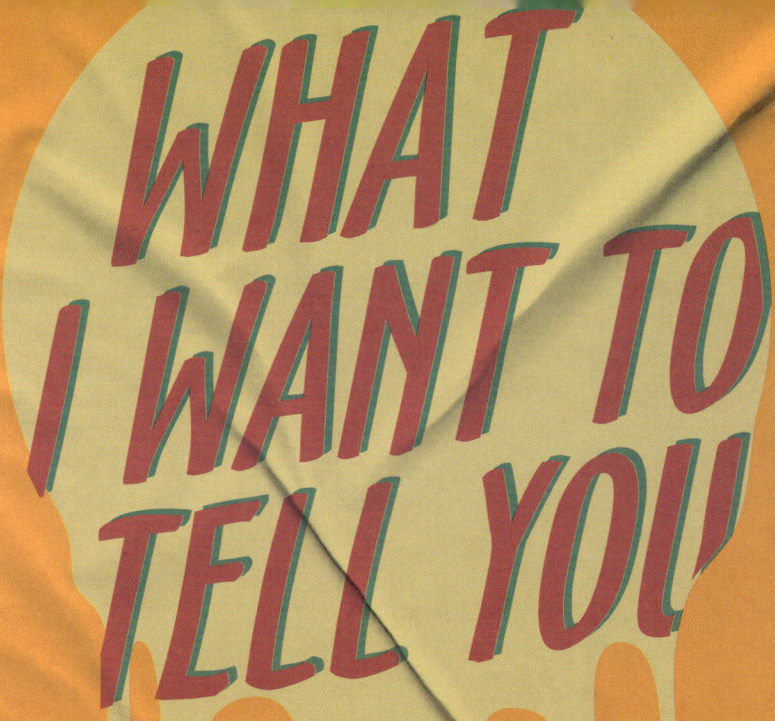

WHAT I WANT TO TELL YOU

Why do we tell each other the stories we do, about ourselves?

What are we trying to say about who we are?

And why do we repeat the same set of stories over and over and over?

What makes a memory live on, at the expense of all other possible memories?

These here are those stories of mine that I have chosen over the years to pluck from the shards of my past—and repeat. These pieces now polished up—to be placed against the black velvet of my full and hidden history.

In each, I am wanting to tell you something about myself. Strung together, the pieces form a pattern—to paint a certain portrait of the self as it wants to be seen.

What singular event seems to vibrate with particular meaning for the teller—and what makes the audience respond with pleasure to the tales so told?

If the listener responds to the teller's tale, he does so out of sympathetic resonance. Some chord that strikes a note of recognition or reflection. So, once told—when received—the tale is no longer about me. *It is about you...*

What m...

memor...

ive on, a...

the expen...

of all othe...

possible

memories?

1 PLAYING WITH FIRE

❋ I'M GONNA BURN YOUR BUSH ❋

In Sierra Leone, the elephant grass turns to parchment in the bleached heat of the dry season. Eight-foot columns of tinder waiting for a friendly match...

Down by the reservoir, my brother and I would run wild looking for toads to spear, lizards to shoot, snakes to chase, birds to startle, ant columns to kick, butterflies to net—while the hawks circled and spied in the bright blue sky.

Not much beats the excitement of running pell-mell through the crackling, bursting grass when it rages up—whipped by the wind—into a galloping roar of sparks and flame. And nothing much beats inhaling that sweet rich smell of the smoke as it billows back and forth before and around us, obscuring, revealing, obscuring, revealing, with sudden jets of oily black then coiled clouds of gray. Fun as good as sex, at least for a kid.

Who knows whether we ever really jump-started a bush fire or two—just for the hell of it? I like to think so. I do know, for sure, we loved to play in that burning bush...

Fun too, were the kill-parties in the clearings beyond the grass. When the fire jumped forward, every hidden critter had to dash for safety—or be roasted alive.

But on the perimeter lurked machete-wielding, stick-poised villagers, looking to stock their dinner pots...

Every kind of crawling, wriggling creature would pour out from the edges of the fire, to be met with cries of exultation, the thump-thump of blades and staffs slicing and raining down on them.

Few would escape.

And those few would most likely find themselves suddenly skewered in the claws of a hawk, soon high in the sky and squirming in their final, bug-eyed moments.

A giant iguana to my young eyes once belted out in all its multi-colored magnificence, to meet a majestic death in a circle of flashing knives. This I found wrenching—and paused me in my delight.

YOUR CAR'S ON FIRE

The Buick Century belched to a stop on red. Fairview and University, in a scarred section of St. Paul. Gray, squat blocks, gray road, gray sky. A lousy nothing of a day. The boat-sized beater's peeled and washed-out greenish paint job fit right in: drab-on-drab. *Easy Does It* cautioned the sticker on the rear. Don't think too hard, don't think too much at all...

She honked.

Head fixed forward, my eyes slid to the right. I didn't take in the color, make and model that revved beside me. Sagging skin, distressed blonde hair, bright red lips—the lady was mouthing and waving at me.

I twisted over and cranked down the window. Gust of sharp cold. And an oily, smoky stench…

"Excuse me," she yelled, "did ya know your car's on fire?"

I craned by neck over the door—fatty tongues of dirty yellow licked up at me from below.

"No, I didn't ma'am. Thank you."

Her eyes hardened, she hesitated, shook her head and accelerated out of my life.

I leapt out and yanked open the hood. The oil cap was missing-in-action. A black slick had spilled across the cowling. And at some point, the oil had just lit itself up.

Perhaps fortunately, the flames flickered out while I stood there watching and wondering…

Robert Fulghum told a story about firefighters who rescued a man from a burning bed. As the firefighters heaved him off the mattress, he remarked, "It was on fire when I lay down on it."

Myself, I have lain down—just way too many times—on burning beds. But a burning car? Just this once.

ULD ESCAPE

FROM TOYS TO TAR

There's a special magic as a child to setting fire to things you love.

Squatting on the garage concrete at four years old, I watched in fascination as my plastic truck went up in smoke. From a garish paint job to a syrupy, black tar that oozed into a satisfying puddle...

My reverie was pierced by my brother's cries: "Mummy, Mummy, Richie's burning his toys!"

A mother's fear and rage in the sands of the Kalahari...

Dad showed up in the late afternoon from his shift in the diamond mine.

"Beat him, John! Beat him!" was the greeting from my mom.

All Dad really wanted when he got home was an affectionate hug and a stiff whiskey—not some ritualized child abuse... I sensed his reluctance—which mitigated some of the pain—as he broke a couple of rulers on my little white butt.

BURNING DOWN THE HUT

Winchester, England. Pre-prep school days. Seven years old. The landlady Fleurette had a garden hut in her back yard. I loved the smell of soil and rotting vegetation mixed with the metallic scent of tools and a beat-up lawnmower.

Jammed against the back was a broke-down desk full of seed packets, yellowed newspaper clippings, thick garden gloves, boxes of matches and other junk.

Now, this all would make for a pretty good blaze....
I piled up a bunch of twigs and clippings and flammable bits and pieces on top of the desk. The first three matches were damp and fizzled with

a smear of blue flame. The fourth match did the trick. I skedaddled as a cheerful blaze took hold. Shortly after, billows of black smoke started to pour from the hut's door—accompanied by screams of alarm from the landlady.

Fleurette quizzed me. I denied everything—despite my obvious guilt.

Upstairs after the interview, I got my just reward—writhing around on the carpet, shielding myself from the blows and furious shrieks of my dear mother.

We had been due to go on an excursion to the Tower of London, to see the Black Prince's armor, the dungeons and the torture devices... Not anymore.

Sandy was n
share her e
and banged
with my re

BRUSHES WITH GREATNESS 2

Peter Bloch of 24 Frames distributed my films in the early seventies— and I sometimes reviewed his various underground offerings for *Time Out* magazine. One evening in '71, Peter spooled out a stateside piece called *Robert Having His Nipple Pierced*.

About 45 minutes—shot in a white-on-white, high-ceilinged room, with Andy Warhol silver pillows floating up and down. Front and center, a half-naked gentleman, propped in the arms of his lover. Some balding, pretend doctor ham-fistedly pierces the young man's left nipple. A bottle of booze is passed backwards and forwards. A hypnotic voice lays down a compelling monologue of reminiscences, anxieties and literary raves.

The movie was cool in its one-stare Warhol way, but it was the relentless monologue that grabbed me by the balls and wouldn't let go. My biggest take away: I got to hear about the flamboyant French writer Blaise Cendrars—whom the narrator had been so inspired by.

I was heading to the States for July and August, so Peter suggested I look up the movie's director Sandy Daley, in New York. Sandy lived on the tenth floor of Hotel Chelsea.

Sandy and I hit it off and she invited me to stay. But no sex. She was recovering from hepatitis. I would have rammed on in regardless, but Sandy was not about to share her egg-yolk eyes and banged-up liver with my reckless desire.

Every day the movie's voice, Patti Smith and the movie's nipple man, Robert Mapplethorpe would swing by. Patti was always so serious. Never saw her cut a smile. Hip coolness reigned. I didn't connect with her much. In hindsight, I should have thanked her for turning me on to Blaise Cendrars. That might have opened the gates a little.

Later, I reviewed the film for *Time Out* and arranged for a photo of her to be placed on the front cover. A famous shot in the end—a half-naked Patti swinging a hammer. Got a friendly note from her after that: "Hey, thanks for splashing my tits all over your magazine."

Robert was a sweetie. Attentive, kind, solicitous... One day he suggested I walk down the block to his loft—so he could show me his artwork. His pieces inserted themselves into my brain. On entering his passageway, a very well-photographed, carefully-composed shot of four male buttholes said hello. The second art piece was a pair of men's briefs stretched tightly on a small white canvas. I made some cool, hip, appreciative noises and the rest is a blur...

✳ BEFORE HER MURDER ✳

I met the precocious and ever-mischievous Julian Allason at Aix-en-Provence, where we were both pretending to study French literature and philosophy. Julian wangled press passes for both of us from the *Daily Mail* to the Cannes Film Festival in May 1968. Not too shabby for a 17-year old. Turns out he'd got his break with a fortuitous photo of Keith Richards and Anita Pallenberg in Chelsea that outed their relationship which turned some heads at the rag—and Bob's Your Uncle.

A nice intro: watching the Cannes screening of *Yellow Submarine*, with all four of the Beatles sitting in the row behind us.

The highlight: Julian photographing Roman Polanski with Sharon Tate in his hotel room. (Julian claimed to have shot Brigitte Bardot at Cannes also but I sure don't recall such a happy moment.)

Roman quickly dispensed with the two teenagers and began jabbering away on the phone, in three languages.

The beautiful and ethereal Sharon Tate led us out onto the balcony over-looking the beach. We discussed astrology and related New Age subject matter in a dreamy kind of way...

Just 13 months later, members of the Charlie Manson gang butchered the heavily-pregnant Tate. It was one of those watershed moments, like Altamont that seemed to signal the transition to a nastier, more fraught and angrier culture. Beads and flowers went out the window in favor of blades and guns.

To draw a line from the Cannes balcony visit to her grisly end in Hollywood, takes a wrenching stroke of the pen.

Our Cannes Film Festival shenanigans ended abruptly just a few days later, when Jean-Luc Godard, Francois Truffaut and Claude Lelouch successfully agitated to have the event shut down, in solidarity with the revolting workers and student protesters. Time to tear up cobblestones, burn cars and get gassed and clubbed by De Gaulle's gendarmes...

I had lunch that winter in London with Julian, his mom and his younger brother Rupert Allason. Rupert later became a military historian, a Conservative MP and the author of numerous books on espionage, under the pen name Nigel West. A smiling brightness and effervescent wit is how I remember both of them.

WANT SOME COCAINE?

Donald Cammell and Nicolas Roeg made the cult film, *Performance*, starring Mick Jagger, James Fox and Anita Pallenberg. In 1970, I interviewed Donald for *Time Out*— the beginning of an intense connection that flared and finally fizzled after six or so months.

One day, Donald invited me to an event. Turned out to be Keith Richards' birthday party at Olympic Studios. The Stones were jamming away at *Sticky Fingers* with friends like Eric Clapton. George Harrison floated around looking majestic, while London's gilded youth circled each other with cool nonchalance.

A long trestle table sagged under some fine treats—including plates of dark chocolate hash cookies. I munched on a few...

Later, dazed and buzzed, I wandered back toward the recording booth. Donald was lying on the floor with an amused lady staring up at me— Bianca Jagger. She extended a hand. "Want some cocaine, John?" First person who had ever offered me uptown... I was off to a good start.

My ride enhanced, I headed into the booth itself, sat down on the couch and listened to the wall of sticky-fingered sound. I felt a hip touch mine. It was Mr. Mick, in to check it out. He gave me his beatific, big-lipped smile and we sat back together for a while, as the music washed over us. I can still see his happy, appreciative, attentive profile as we listened to the rich, evocative, pounding beats that defined my soul that night.

MASTER LOU

As a 19-year old undergraduate at Cambridge, I picked up a copy of *The Velvet Underground and Nico*, followed by *White Light, White Heat*. These two albums celebrate drug addiction, polymorphous sexuality and every manner of deviant behavior. They also contain incandescent lyrics, a burning soulfulness and a brilliantly visceral music that is timeless in its impact. Wild to the bone—with a haunting resonance that reverberates within me to this day.

Not long after, the artist-in-residence at Kings College, Cambridge, Mark Lancaster, gave me a note of introduction to his friends Ted Hughes and Andy Warhol. Which led me to hanging out at the Factory and meeting Lou Reed at Max's Kansas City.

It was a tough time for Lou's band. One night it was just me and my girlfriend dancing in front of the Velvets, with an impassive Jonas Mekas the sole audience.

40 years after we first met, Lou re-entered my life, through our mutual passion for Chen Tai Chi. Through a shared lineage, I met him at a Tai Chi seminar in New York, then on a short film project in St. Paul where Lou acted opposite my daughter, Nicole.

Legend has it, he died doing Tai Chi, with his eyes open, held by his wife, Laurie Anderson, a look of rapture on his face. From the imprisoning seduction of heroin to the blissful flow of subtle qi, the release is complete.

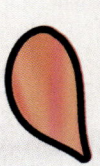

COBRA BLOOD AND A SHOT OF SCOTCH

Sam Robards is an actor and a physical culturist. His dad was Jason Robards, his mum Lauren Bacall. Sam got certified as a kettlebell instructor and came to a flexibility workshop taught by me, Pavel and Steve Maxwell.

Sam was cool. While eating at an Indian restaurant in Minneapolis we shared stories about the wildest things we'd ever eaten. Like wasps, baby scorpion and locusts.

Sam had a good story, but he was gun shy on the full reveal.

While filming in Thailand, he had visited a street shack selling cobra blood. A certain A-list star was part of the party…

The young Thai server jammed a wriggling cobra onto a large nail that stuck out from a dark-stained beam. Sliced the body open from the neck. Caught the gush of blood in a beer glass—then splashed in a generous shot of Scotch.

The movie star grabbed the glass and chugged the entire contents in a few gurgly gulps. There was a pause. Then: "Gaaaaarrrggghhh!" He spewed the entire contents all over his mates at the table…

Sam refused to name the star.

Some years later, I was watching Brian de Palma's formidable movie, *Casualties of War*, based on the true story of a group of Marines abducting, raping and murdering a young Vietnamese villager. Suddenly up popped Sam—as the military pastor hearing a stammered confession from Michael J. Fox.

And I had my answer. Sean Penn.

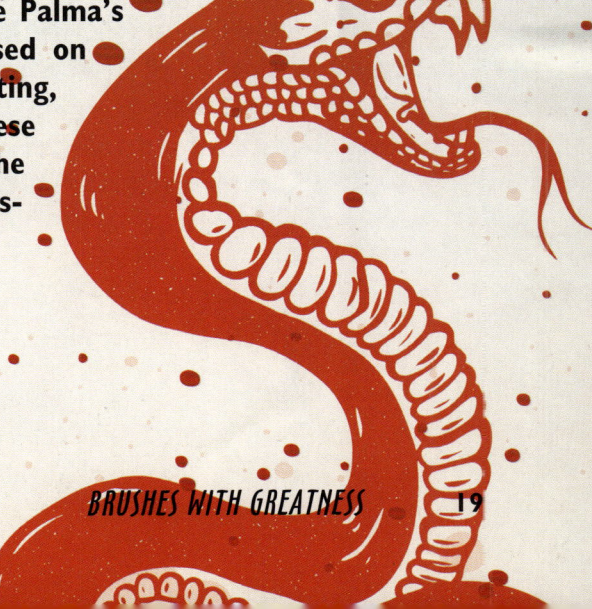

THE LATTER DAY LUNCH

In 1971, the obscure Canadian film maker Kris Patterson invited a group of high-ego types to sit around an open-air feast, sip champagne, drive rolled banknotes across mirrors caked with coke—and fire up an endless supply of hash-laden spliffs.

Twelve of us each pontificated for a few minutes in a deliberately self-important manner on a subject most dear to our self-involved hearts...

The most notable—and most understated—of the group was Donovan. Our over-the-top punkster posturing ground the gears of his gentle, flower-child spirit—and he took off to a corner of the lawn, to play guitar with his wife Linda Lawrence. (Linda had previously been with Brian Jones and had had a kid, Julian with him.)

Kris spliced in clips of carnage from the streets of Belfast by way of ironic commentary. The result was *The Latter Day Lunch*—one of those bizarre shorts that crawl from the cutting room to a single showing and then disappear without trace.

Kris came to a grisly end—straight out of a David Cronenberg movie. His drunken head was bashed in at a motel by this beautiful, pill-popping psychopath. He had met the lady on an art counseling gig at a Canadian psychiatric hospital. Kris had wangled a weekend pass for her to accompany him to that rendezvous.

She fled the scene—and Kris lay there for several days before they found him...

ANGER RISING

While at Cambridge I became obsessed with underground cinema—even forming a film society to show early Warhol movies like *Chelsea Girls*—which required simultaneous projection of two reels side by side.

Tony Rayns was a fellow undergraduate and by far the most influential film critic of us all. Tony in particular worshipped the brilliant shorts by Kenneth Anger—and did his poor best to emulate them in his own film work. I respected Anger's work, but the black magic and the homo-eroticism were not for me.

However, after Donald Cammell introduced me to Anger in the late seventies, we shared some memorable moments. Donald's mother had been a close friend of Aleister Crowley—a major inspiration for Kenneth...

I got to watch *Lucifer Rising* and various works in progress at Anger's apartment. I will never forget the sight of Marianne Faithful smacked out of her gourd, slowly climbing up an absurdly steep Celtic stone stairway cut into a mountain. And then there was Bobby Beausoleil, the unapologetic Manson cohort and celebrity murderer...

The hip fascination with Devil worship seemed childish, naïve and mistaken, to my mind—which was more attuned to a Buddhist approach to life. But Anger had an endearing intensity about him that, for me, balanced out the mania.

After a numb

hallucinatory

we heade

to bed.

ACID IN MY TEA

For a brief and gorgeous time, I went out with the super-talented and altogether-special Penny Slinger. Penny dripped sex. A mystical surrealist with a penchant for the sublimely erotic, she went on with Nik Douglas to produce the seminal *Sexual Secrets*—which helped initiate the modern Tantra movement.

I met the straight-laced parents at her art show. Mom and Dad looked politely pained. I think the wedding cake—with its engorged penises thrusting up from the white icing—might have set them off a little...

One of Penny's girlfriends asked, "So... the million-dollar question... did Penny use yours as the model?"

"I'm not that small..."

Just before we hooked up, Penny had acted in a histrionic, acid-laced shambles of a movie, *The Other Side of the Underneath*, directed by Jane Arden. I found it relentlessly repellent. But that didn't stop me from being massively attracted to its beautiful star.

Over Christmas, Penny invited me to share an evening with Sally the sad-faced cellist from *Underneath*. In the kitchen, the ladies served me tea and we chatted idly about this and that. At some point the light began to bend and colors to bleed and swell. They had spiked my tea with acid. Big time. Shades of the movie...

After a number of hallucinatory hours, we headed to bed. I have never been a fan of threesomes—in any of the versions I've been involved in. I treasure deep intimacy and communion with one person. I've always found the dynamic of a third wheel to be awkward. The acid blurred some of the edges this time round—but still not my cuppa...

THE ANGRY DWARF FROM HORROR HOSPITAL

Have you ever had a character from a horror movie suddenly show up for real in front of you? I have. I blame Antony Balch.

1973, Tony invited me to a screening of his *Horror Hospital* which I reviewed with irreverence in *Time Out*. My favorite character in the movie was a bizarre dwarf, Frederick, hammed up to the hilt by Skip Martin. I forget my exact phrasing, but I used some wildish words to describe Skip's performance.

Shortly after the review hit, I was hunching over my Olivetti on the top floor office of *Time Out*, when I sensed a presence to my right...

The crazed dwarf from *Horror Hospital* stood before me, angry, waving his arms in front of my face. Skip pitched me a load, hammering my insensitivity to dwarf-people. My ill-considered choice of phrasing had come across as prejudice.

"Frederick" was kind enough not to slit my throat, as he had so happily done to the hippies in the hospital. I invited him for a drink at a nearby pub and he filled me in on his fascinating past, acting in everything from Otto Preminger's *Saint Joan* to Roger Corman's *The Masque of the Red Death*.

Tony died of stomach cancer at the age of 42. Besides *Horror Hospital* I owe him for having introduced me to William Burroughs at his apartment on Duke Street. Tony had labored for years to get Bill's *Naked Lunch* turned into a movie, with Mick Jagger as the star. Fortunate, really, that the project foundered—so that later David Cronenberg could do it the justice it deserved.

PAST LIVES, PRESENT LIVES

3

MEETING ADONIS AT THE CROSSROADS

John Schofill had been a nuclear engineer, until he downed enough acid to scramble his science and flip to the role of starry-eyed underground filmmaker. I met John in Berkeley, on a summer vacation from Cambridge.

"John, you've got a very spiritual face—I'd like you to star as the Soul in my film on the *Tibetan Book of the Dead*." I think it helped that I had shoulder-length hair, a raggedy beard and a yellow Indian shirt with red mantras painted across it.

"Sure, Paul, when do we start?"

Paul and I road-tripped to the Four Corners region, where at one point I found myself spread-eagled buck naked hanging from a cliff at dawn, thinking "I don't remember this being part of the *Tibetan Book of the Dead*—and what in hell am I doing here?"

Done with the shoot, Paul dropped me on the edge of Berkeley and I hitched out a coupla hundred miles to a desert crossroads.

A lone figure stood with his thumb out. Damn! It was Tony Meyers, an actor friend of mine from Cambridge. Didn't even know the bugger was in the States...

Tony's clean-cut, Adonis profile and buff physique got us to New York in three days flat. He would do the thumbing—and I would lurk in the shadows. When the hopeful victim pulled up, I would scuttle from behind my rock and join the band.

Like writing on water, there is an indecipherable beauty to the mysteries of these spooky meetings. How can they be? It's as if there was an invisible network of souls seeking each other out again and again—to reconnect and rework past karma.

DO YOU HAVE A SISTER— AND IS YOUR DAD A BUTCHER?

On my gap year before Cambridge, my high school roommate and I toured Europe in the Summer in his beat-up little van. We camped on the outskirts of Istanbul for a few days where we met this wild-eyed, English hippie who raved at a mile a minute about two things: his overland trip to India and the beautiful ladies of Copenhagen. My timid, bespectacled, Welsh travel companion was afraid to cross the Bosphorous, but he was up for checking out the action in Denmark. So on impulse, we tossed our previous plans and headed north to the beckoning Scandinavian babes. You make decisions like that when you are seventeen.

Despite all the hoopla, I found it frustratingly hard to get laid in this supposed den of iniquity and easy ladies. Perhaps my youth betrayed me... but, tough sledding—tough, tough sledding. Truth be grudgingly told, my one good time was with a thirty-something woman who had a thing for teenage boys, I guess.

My musical passion then was the jazz of John Coltrane, Archie Shepp, Ornette Coleman, Roland Kirk and the like. I used to hit the London jazz spots, like Ronnie Scott's, hard—and followed the same program in Copenhagen.

A radiant, fresh-faced blonde showed up also almost every night at the Jazzhus Montmartre, my favorite hangout. I did my best to entice her into something more, but it was not to be…

The closest it ever got was a visit to our apartment the night before I left for London. Her boyfriend was away in Yugoslavia. I sensed an opportunity. We lay in bed staring at each other, holding each other, but that was all she wrote.

Seven years later, in 1975, I was doggedly pursuing enlightenment at the Bhagwan Rajneesh ashram in Poona, India. I had rented a spacious apartment nearby. In the Tai Chi class, a red-haired Danish lady was a dedicated co-student. Her girlfriend was sharing my apartment. She asked me if the Danish lady could move in to the vacant room. Sure…

Six months later, Danish and I were sitting opposite each other in the kitchen, sharing a juice. Something jogged in me. I looked at her intently then asked, "Do you have a sister—and is your dad a butcher?"

The veils dropped and we recognized each other. It was my friend from the Jazzhus Monmartre.

✳ I WAS STRANGLED AT BIRTH ✳

Exasperated at not having achieved enlightenment in my previous life, I organized with my mother this time around to be strangled at birth.

Really, I should have been hacked out of her. It would have saved us both from a lifetime of later heartache. See, I had lain inside her canal for two days with the umbilical cord double-wrapped around my throat, strangling while she pushed in vain to get me out of her. The technical term is nuchal cord and it only occasionally leads to brain damage or death. But all the fetal-me could figure was that an attempted murder was in process.

What were those South African medics up to—leaving me in there, tangled, choking, desperate, while my mother writhed in her own pain hour after hour after hour? I'd wanted to make a statement and they most certainly complied with the request…

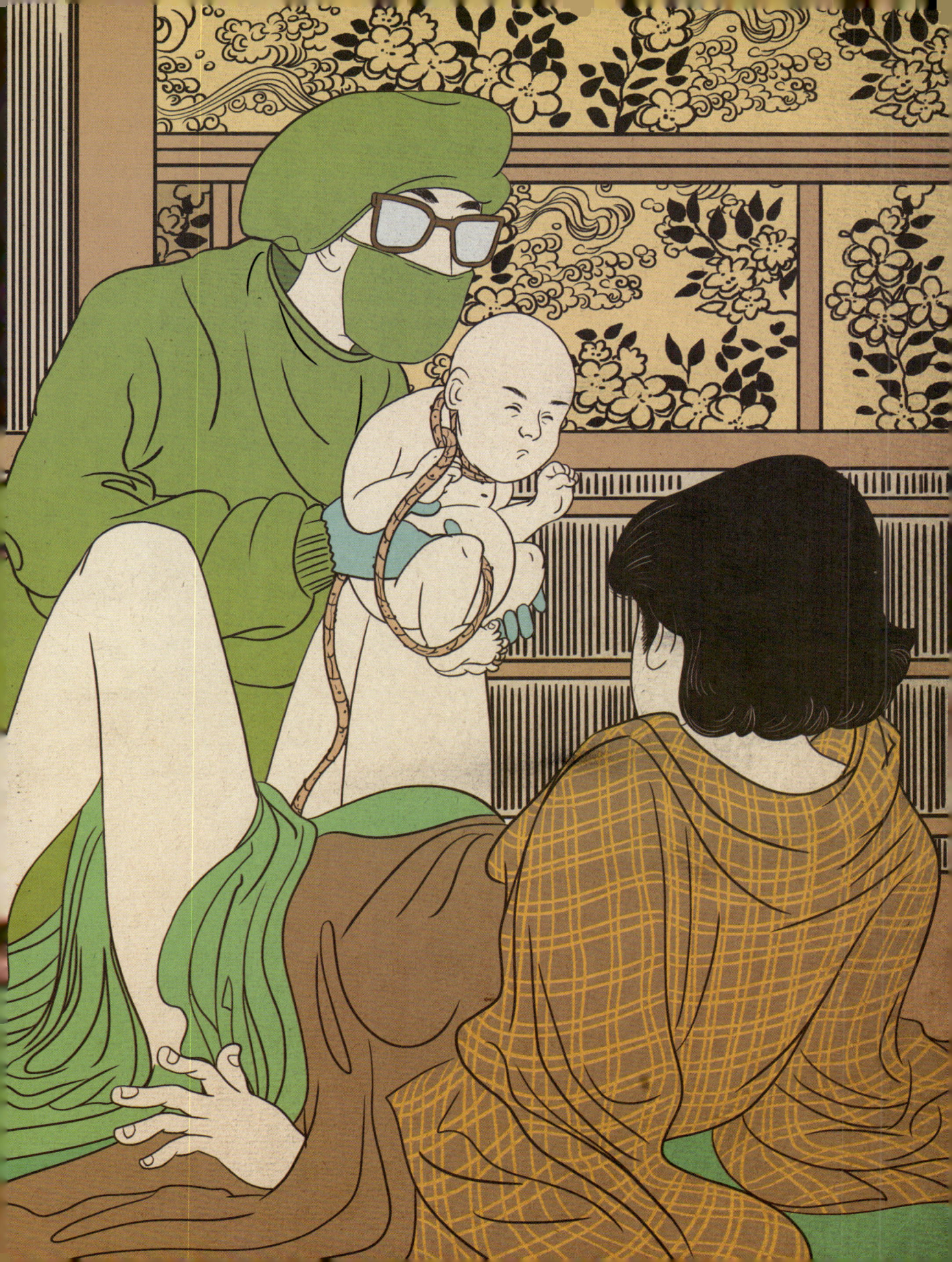

When they finally yanked me from her bloody chamber and they raised my head to her face, I gave her a furious, accusatory glare—or so she told me later. In her late eighties, not long before she died, she'd said to me suddenly one day, "It wasn't my fault." My mother's look at the memory of it seemed to stretch new lines on her old skin—while her pleading eyes, with their yearning for reciprocated love, betrayed the hurt that had lingered for a lifetime.

The strangulation had consequences beyond the fraught beginnings with my mother. Wearing a necktie is something I avoid at all costs. I used to joke that in a previous life I had been hanged—hence the discomfort at the feeling of constriction. Perhaps, but for maximum immediate impact let's just look back in anger and fear at that birth experience. And I've struggled for a lifetime with a narrow windpipe that can have me gasping for air, heart hammering, as I clutch with a start at my throat in the middle of the night.

Mostly though, the event has played out as an excessive quest for independence and freedom—which has so often flipped into its very opposite, restriction and a kind of bondage. That—and a curious ambivalence about continuing to live this life as I have created it for myself.

DRUG-OLOGY

4

✳ BASE COCAINE AND THE BLUE LIGHT ✳

In the mid-nineties, I promoted Terry Dunn's *Flying Phoenix Qigong*—a super-potent system he had absorbed from the mysterious Grandmaster Doo Wai. Calibrated sequences of breath-holding, combined with esoteric postures, induced a flood of qi and sometimes altered states—even a feeling of transcendent bliss.

After a seminar I hosted in St. Paul, Terry told me a Doo Wai story. While training Terry and his fellow students in a hotel room, Wai asked, "Would you like to see the color of qi?"

Wai flicked the lights off. Moments later, a blue glow issued from his hands, bathing the agape students in a ghostly glimmer. An odor as of singed flesh— then a slow fade to darkness… I wondered at the time, "Could this really have happened?" But then I got jerked back to a curiously similar experience I'd had in a Los Angeles motel in the late seventies.

"WOULD YOU LIKE TO SEE THE COLOR OF QI?"

I was holding a blow torch to this glass container of base cocaine. As the wicked vapors rose from the melting shards, I sucked them up into my eager lungs. Held those vapors until they entered my blood and my heart pounded and my brain sang on the edge of climax. King for a fleeting moment—king of it all—until the inevitable slide back into neediness and the anxious craving for more and more and more.

Hollywood Henry sat hunched opposite in an armchair, long legs and bony knees spread wide, as I checked his doctored Peruvian...

Then, Zang! I felt this jolt in my left shoulder. Then a pulsing sensation... this blue light shooting down my arm, pooling in my palm—then issuing in a stream from my fingers.

Was I hallucinating?

"Henry, did you just see something?"

Henry arched his right eyebrow. "Yup." He described exactly what I had felt and seen. The same vivid issuing of the blue light—a monstrous, cum-like discharge of my precious essence into the murky motel air.

"John," a friend commented sadly to me shortly after, "you're like a container that has had its spigots wrenched open until almost every drop of energy has been drained out." And I remember Chaka Khan bursting into tears at the sight of my haggard, wrecked, depleted self when we reconnected in a New York coffee shop after some months apart. Years of careful qi cultivation had been dissipated in the blind chase of an ever-receding promise of bliss. It would be another fifteen years before I would return to the slow and patient process of restoring that energy, through such practices as Flying Phoenix Qigong and the like.

We build beauty. We destroy the beauty. We rebuild the beauty. And so it goes...

SEX-CAPADES 5

✳ HOW TO SURVIVE BEING RAPED BY A BEATNIK ✳

When you are sixteen years old and hanging out at clubs like UFO, on 31 Tottenham Court Road, London—to watch the house bands Pink Floyd and The Soft Machine—you can end up the night in some surprising places...

One fine evening, a short, bearded forty-something beatnik siddled up beside me and began to wheedle in a confiding, natural, easy, humorous way. I went along with his banter. I was on a mission. "Know where I could score some hash?" I asked him. He suggested we try another club I liked to visit, The Roaring Twenties, on 50 Carnaby Street. Lots of West Indians and Africans there and great music. Just had to stay out of the random knife fight, punch up or half-hearted police raid...

The built West Indian gentleman who sold us the hunk of hash came back with us to the beatnik's squalid basement flat. He rolled up a massive spliff and we started passing it around. The pungent blend of tobacco and dope smoke began to mask the ambient smell of stale urine and unwashed bodies.

Sucking on that fat spliff with my greedy teenage enthusiasm got me quickly in over my head. Dizziness. Head throbbing, then a heaving and convulsing from the gut. Bile belched up into my throat. Nasty. And spacy. "Hey, I need to lie down!" I slumped down onto the ratty couch with its burst springs and torn, stained fabric.

Then this from the West Indian: "So, who's going to be the bigger beast?" Who got to do the poor wee lad lying there defenseless kind of in his stupor? Thankfully, the beatnik pressed his prior claim and the dealer took off.

Next thing I knew, the beatnik was squirming around on top of me. I barfed all over the floor. A fresh, bitter stench rose up to compete with the smorgasbord of stinks. My dinner lay in yellow chunks across the carpet. While Scruffman cleaned it up, I crawled off into the middle of the room.

But the vomit was no deterrent. Back on top of me he went, begging me to do him… somehow, he got his infested mouth on mine for a moment, before I could twist away. I threw up again. When he ran to mop up a second time, I staggered to my feet and bolted out and into the street, followed by forlorn cries of "Come back, come back!"

Back home at my oblivious parents, I bent over the basin and retched again as the clammy memory played itself out in my flesh. I have seldom ever felt quite that soiled and dirty. My skin crawled. My ashen mug stared back at me from the mirror.

This little escapade had some dramatic consequences. Shortly after, I came down with raging gingivitis—the swollen, pus-laden gums a final exclamation mark to memorialize that sordid encounter. I had a fun day at the dentist having my gums cut back. Fresh, light-pink tissue grew back up, but a curious vulnerability has remained in place. You can cut away the flesh all you want, but the phantom lives on regardless…

JACKIE BE GOOD

One night I was sitting in the backroom of Max's Kansas City with Taylor "Lonesome Cowboy" Mead, when Jackie Curtis flounced up and sat down to my right. Jackie had written an off-off-Broadway play in which she also starred. It must have been *Vain Victory: Vicissitudes of the Damned*. She was fresh from the show, in full dress costume, with silver glitter on her rouged cheeks. Buzzed and still fully in her role. Queen Jackie.

"Jackie, this is John" offered Taylor with that sly, endearing grin of his. "Hello, John." Jackie held my gaze—as her hand slid to my groin and started to stroke my junk. I got hard. With my hardness in complete control of my brain, I blurted "Let's go to your place." Jackie pulled back, startled. A casual shock-tease-come-on—met with an offer. "Uh, okay." She rose to the challenge.

We headed out and jumped into a Yellow. In the back seat, I stared at Jackie's left-side profile. In the harshest of harsh late-night street lighting, coarse man-stubble showed through Jackie's make up. Damn, I was in some pickle of my own making... I had zero interest in sex with any kind of male—and most certainly not with this thick-set, hairy guy. Damn, damn, but oh well, what the hell.

Locked and loaded the trigger had been squeezed. We headed uptown to Jackie's apartment. This beautiful, smiling, inviting Indian actress met us at the door. The roommate. Could there be a last-moment switch here, I prayed? Wasn't going to happen.

Jackie was good-natured and kind. She did her best to get me excited despite my clearly wilted outlook. I made a valiant effort to fulfill my promise but it sure would have been nice if I could have mustered up some genuine desire. "You're so big," she purred as I topped her, but I wasn't too fooled and simply couldn't stay hard for her. "Yeah, right," I thought as I stared down at my half-inflated thing.

Jackie took my inability to get properly aroused in stride. We parted on friendly enough terms... Next time we were together at Max's she

looked at me, leaned over and whispered into a friend's ear, smirking. They chuckled for a moment. A faint smile most likely flitted across my face, before I picked up my hamburger and took a bite...

Ah, Jackie, she died so young, blue in the face, of a heroin overdose at age 38. Another great talent laid waste by addiction.

Whenever I hear that *Walk on the Wild Side* line "Jackie thought she was James Dean for a day", I remember this interlude. And I smile again, the lines crinkling in the skin beside my eyes.

YOU WANT BEAUTIFUL LADY COME?

The Chinese authorities send mixed messages about sex work. Almost every spa and massage place seems to offer more than just therapeutic services. It is prevalent enough that you might assume it was legal. It's not. The powers appear to let things ride, then every now and then stomp down hard. Sometimes very hard: one gentleman recently got sentenced to death for running a prostitution ring in Shenzhen...

On one of my first visits to China, I got my introduction to one such set up.

The Sino Swiss Hotel Beijing Airport looked not too bad on the web. But the reality was more than a little sketchy...

I had some time to kill in the morning, so decided to check out the hotel spa. Now, the spa was located straight off the main lobby through a wide-open passage way. No doors.

The massage table was behind a kind of hospital screen. There was draping, but the public could waltz right in, any time they cared to...

The massage was terrific. Solid Tui-na. But near the end, the solid Tui-na started to morph into some subtle, carressive finger-tip work. She was signaling a fresh agenda.

The therapist lent over my face and whispered: "You want beautiful lady come now, give you special massage?"

Well, there is a time and a place for all kinds of hanky panky, right?

But in broad, bright daylight, in plain view to the curious and in a semi-clinical setting—nah, I think I'll pass, thanks.

NOT WITH THE DRIVER, HONEY

In desperate days, struggling to get Dragon Door airborne, I took part-time work as a limo driver. I saw some things… and here's a choice example:

In the shaded glow of a Minnesota summer's evening, I picked up a 3M engineer and his speech-pathologist wife. The engineer had a snickering laugh that issued from him in stuttered bursts of self-involvement. The lady was all woman—luscious, ample and exuding sensuality.

We headed to Minneapolis and picked up an elegant couple—a suave African American doctor and his sweet-faced, blonde partner. Off to dinner after a ride around the lake… through the divider I heard furtive rustlings, grunts and giggles. Sexual scents wafted through the cracks. As I pulled open the door at the restaurant, the blonde gave me an embarrassed, red-faced look as she fumbled to adjust her dress.

On the way to Prince's club Glam Slam, the divider slid down and half of the speech pathologist pushed herself through the gap… "I love you!" she cried, turning toward my neck. "Not with the driver!" shouted her husband, as he yanked her back into the melee behind.

Waiting, as limo drivers wait so much… then 3M dude came scuttling out of the club and asked me to drive him, alone, to a nearby strip club. After a quickie at the strip joint, we bolted back to the oblivious trio at Glam Slam…

"I'm a pervert!" he confided to me with a gleeful cackle as we parted at the end of the night.

IS THIS A DATE?

The Americans invented "dating"—although they are usually puzzled when I tell them so…

It all began with the rise of the automobile in the United States. For the first time, young couples could go out by themselves, unchaperoned, in a car—and have their way with each other: The Date. No such luck for almost all English and Europeans. Relatively car-less and overcrowded, we went out in gangs and mobs, whatever the final intention might be… A generalization, but you get my drift.

When I first moved to Minnesota in 1985, I was constantly thrown by the frequent references to "dating". Was this a straight euphemism for sex? Or something more general? Depended on the person and the situation, it appeared.

I was interested in this one lady and invited her to dinner and a movie. As we drove to the movie, she asked me hesitatingly, "Is this a date?" I was flummoxed … just mumbled something noncommittal.

The conversation turned to her recent divorce. She had left her husband for another person. When I asked who the new guy had been, she clarified that it was a woman—which explained the hesitant question about the date.

We did still end in bed—for a little bit. After a while of gentle caressing and closeness, she looked at me, "John, you appeal to the five percent of me that is attracted to men…"

TO DO—OR NOT DO—DEBBIE DYE

September 1997. My brother Peter was in town with an Aussie crew to film at the Minnesota Zoo for his Malaysian Rainforest series. We arranged to go to Famous Dave's to hear the iconic electric blues artist Joe Louis Walker. Joe was definitely no slouch and had played with everyone from

Jimi Hendrix to Steve Miller to John Mayall, to Steve Miller, to Buddy Guy and Ike Turner. Peter's cameraman, Ian Pugsley, had a stack of Walker albums back home, so we were all stoked to check Joe out. I felt excited to treat my brother and his friends to such special entertainment on their foray into the frozen tundra.

I showed up at Dave's early. A stained wooden table near the front and side seemed open except for this fox at the far end of it. The lady gave me an appraising scan, then flipped her hand to the seat beside her. Introduced herself—in a deeply Southern accent—as Debbie, Debbie Dye. Debbie was one kind of my-kind-of-a-gal. Long, slinky, sensuous body. Dark velvet skin. High cheekbones. A promise in the heavy-lidded eyes. We started to caress each other with small talk and she let me know, casually, that Joe was her boyfriend—when he was in town…

Peter and Ian and the rest of the crew arrived to interrupt our foreplay. It was hilarious watching the Australians trying to make head or tail of what Debbie was saying, a rapid-paced patois that seemed to spill sideways out of her lips. They would nod wisely with glazed looks and have no clue what she was saying—which was just fine.

Boyfriend Joe was blazing away on stage in his magnificent way, drenching us with his fiery riffs. Debbie asked me to dance and who was I to say no and there we were, almost alone in front of the stage, lost in the fierce, insistent rhythms, regardless of how we looked or seemed. I had thrown my mind in the backseat and let my body take the wheel.

At intermission, Joe came to join us, regaled us with stories and hinted at terrible things—at a pain and a suffering that was more then he dared to share, at least with us. There was this temptation to try to match him story for story, to show him that I wasn't some innocent, harmless lad, some cherry boy with little clue about the dark alleys and the sewers and the rats and the piss-stained cobblestones and the graffiti and the tossed needles and the sprawled homeless and the shed blood. But I didn't go there and for good reason.

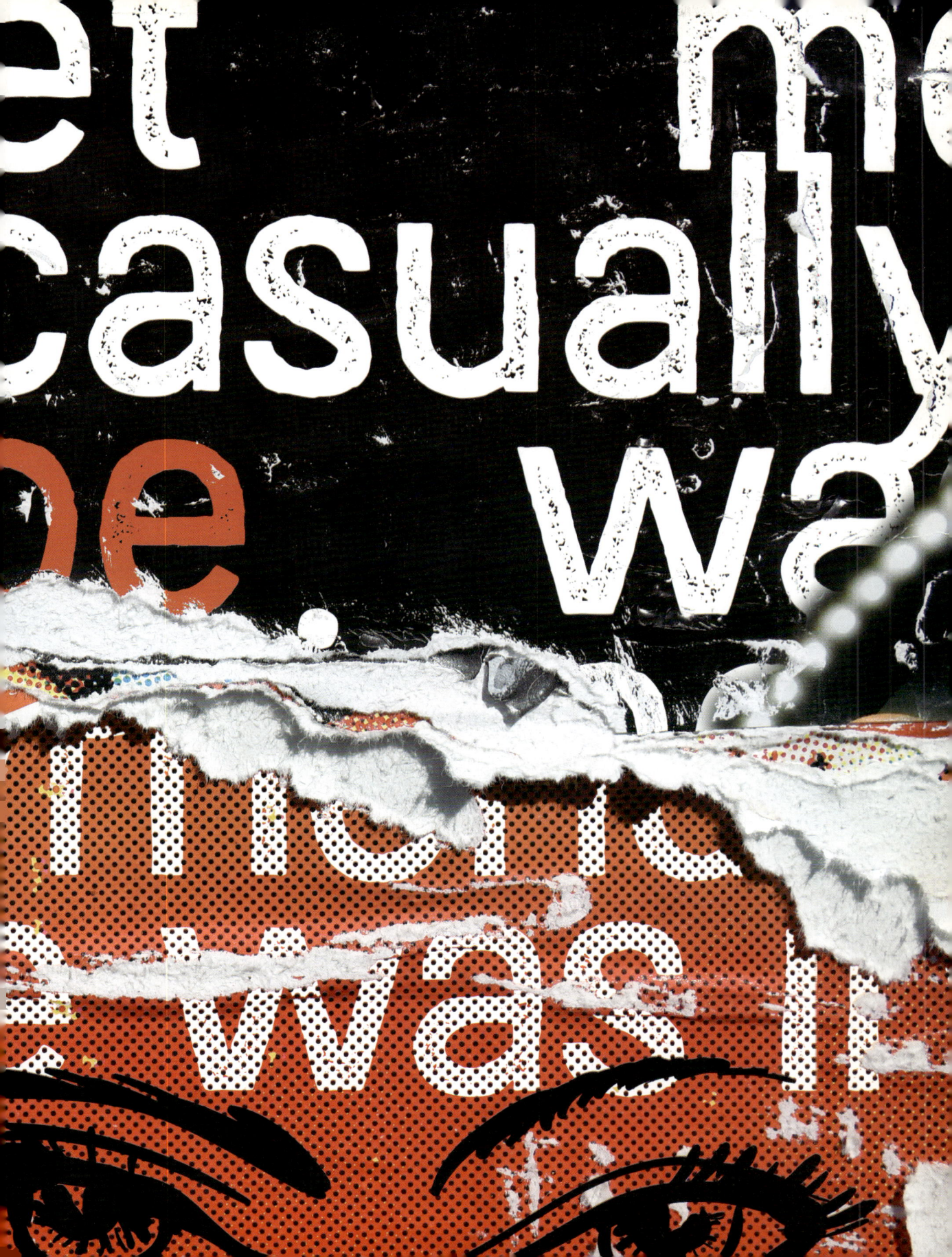

As the final set was coming to its climax, the Aussies signaled their need to beat it, scraping back their chairs, grabbing their coats, taking a last slug of scotch or Guinness or wine or whatever. Debbie tore off a piece of napkin and scribbled down her number and looked me in the eye as she handed me the invite.

Now, in 1997 AIDS was still a death sentence and Bareback was another name for Russian Roulette. Skin-on-skin could cost you your very life, yet protection was like banging on a keyboard with oven mitts. What to do? We played safe, except when we didn't—or couldn't bear to and said damn the torpedoes. Of course, it's still a bum deal—but not quite the old-time chiller with the bony fingers from days past. The odds are still stacked for the House, yes. But you can bullet-dodge and jingle-jangle around for longer now—and breathe a sigh of relief when your bill comes back, temporarily clean. But 1997 was still often a time when my angel refused to rush in, however much my devil tried to goad him on. A warning signal from deep down to control the idiocy of the urge. And Debbie's offer was one of those times when something held me back and I never made the call.

I kept that torn piece of napkin in my pocket for quite some time—in fact until it started to disintegrate and the inky scratchings became indecipherable. I think Debbie's invite finally got laundered away, lost forever in the gray suds of a forgotten wash. I was left with one of those What If's that haunts you through the years. You wonder what you might have missed—or you wonder if there would have been a YOU left alive to wonder what you might have missed…

Debbie, where ARE you now?

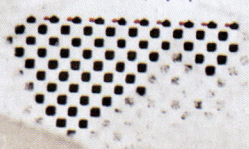

DEBBIE
WHERE
ARE
YOU
NOW?

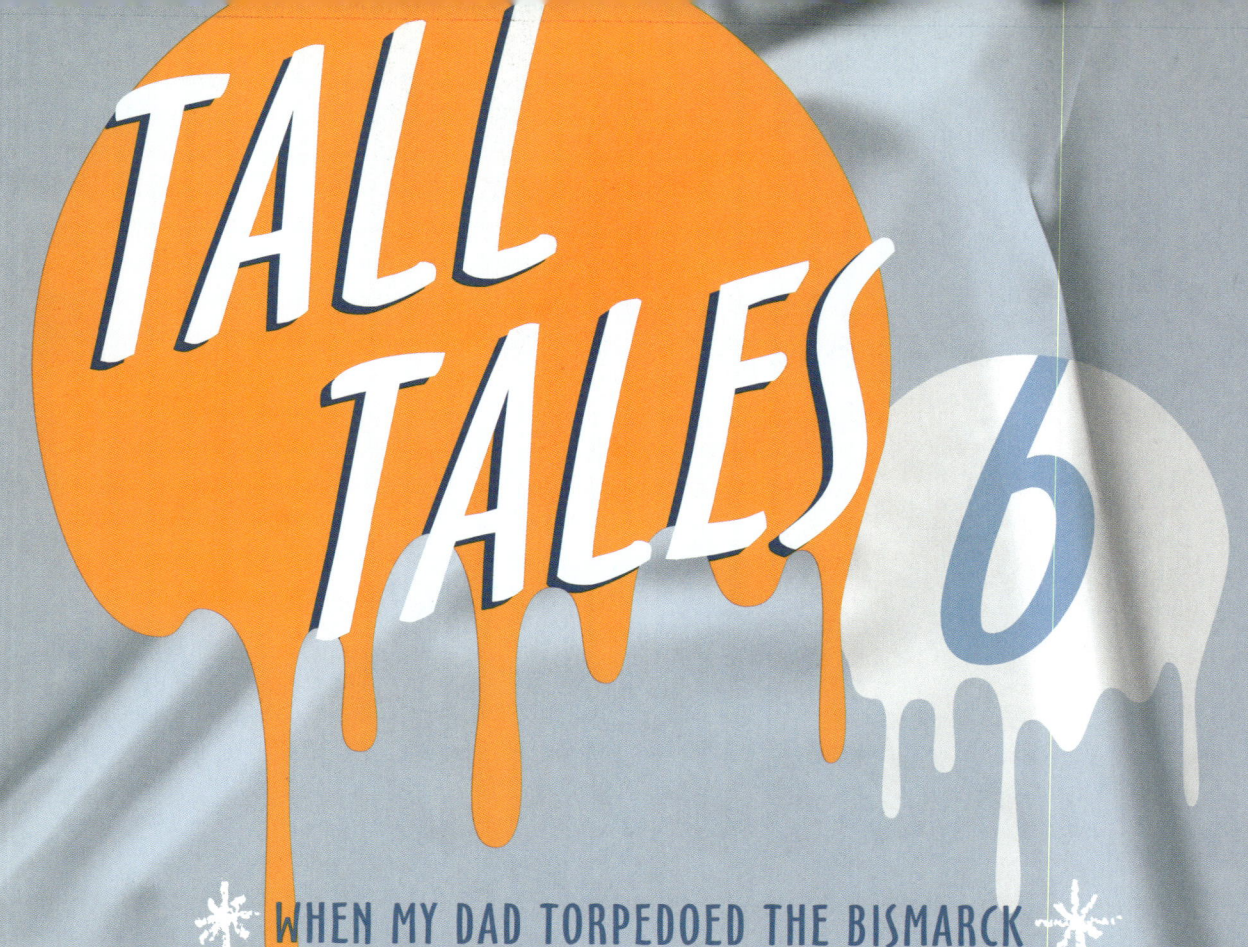

TALL TALES 6

❋ WHEN MY DAD TORPEDOED THE BISMARCK ❋

On May 26th, 1941, my dad took off from the *Ark Royal* aircraft carrier in a Faery Swordfish. His mission: torpedo and sink the Nazi battleship *Bismarck*.

Now imagine: you are flying an ancient bi-plane toward one full side of Germany's most powerful warship. Every gun is blazing away at you. You skim the waves, approaching at approximately 120 mph...

The Swordfish suddenly lightens as the torpedo releases. You rear up and bank away...

And you make it—mostly because your plane flew too slow and low for the gunners' fire-control predictors to nail you.

Safely out of range, you turn to give your observer a smiling thumbs-up. Neither the smile nor the thumbs-up are returned. The poor blighter has lost his head—shot off as the plane banked away. There's just a jagged, bloody neck to greet you back. The rear gunner's helmet is decorated

with a spray of light pink. Perhaps he doesn't even yet know what happened to his mate, as he scans the skies for incoming fighters.

I told this story many times to my children. A hero tale, lionizing their grandpa.

But the story is not exactly accurate. Yes, my dad flew Faery Swordfish torpedo bombers in the Second World War. Yes, the Bismarck was crippled by such an attack on May 26th, 1941.

But he did not participate in this battle. At all... I had taken episodes out of the movie *Sink The Bismarck!* and combined them with photos of my dad at war to create a fresh portrait, lionizing him into legend.

I caught flak from my kids—in particular, my son—for having made up this tale. They feel betrayed, somehow.

But I don't regret the telling of it. It's an embellishment, a wish fulfillment and a measure of how I really saw my dad...

✳ DEATH BY CROCODILE ✳

The red clay roads in the fifties in Sierra Leone would often lead down to a swollen river with no bridge.

Two chains span the river. The chains run either side of a ferry of pontoons, empty gasoline drums and wooden planks. The ferrymen yank on the chains to pull the load across.

In 1957, my parents, my brother and I were waiting to cross by such a ferry. But first an ancient mammy wagon teetered onto

THE ILLUSTRATED WILD BOY

the planks, stuffed with squawking chickens, ladies in a riot of brightly-colored clothing, half-naked, squalling kids…

Downstream were some rocks and rapids with crocodiles basking nearby on the muddy banks…

A snapping sound—like a gunshot. Cries of alarm. One of the chains had broken. The ferry swung around and started to tilt over. A massive crashing and screaming—the hugely over-burdened mammy wagon had toppled over, ejecting its load into the river.

The force of the rapids sucked the mammies and their kids down toward the waiting rocks…

I gazed toward the muddy banks: the crocodiles had disappeared… but wait, there they were, their snouts and eyes and spiny backs gliding toward the oncoming gift of fresh flesh…

Many drowned that day and some were eaten, we later learned.

Shaken, we climbed back into the dusty Land Rover and beat our retreat.

This is another tale told as entertainment for my kids, weaving in some truths with some blatant embellishments.

Everything is true in this story until the point at which the fictionalizer asks the question: "What if one of those chains broke in mid-stream?"

❋ LIKE FATHER, LIKE SON ❋

2:05 am. A polite but firm and insistent knocking on the front door. I drag some clothes on and stumble downstairs. Two boys in blue at the door.

"Are you Peter Du Cane's father?"

"Uh huh…"

"We have your son in the backseat of our car. The good news is that he is okay."

Evidently, 16-year old Peter had just totaled his Camry—ramming it into an RAV 4 that had been parked one street over. Slammed into it with some obvious speed. On a side street—at what, forty or fifty miles per hour?

According to the one officer, Peter had explained how his windshield had been hit by a flying raccoon. The shock of that critter's splutt on the almost shattered glass had caused Peter to swerve into the RAV. The officer did a great acting job delivering this story, his eyes gleaming while the rest of his face remained impassive.

Peter had been hammered. By all rights, the cops should have hauled his sorry ass off for a night in the cells and his first DUI. They described his incoherent attempts to recite the alphabet and count backwards while standing on one leg and so on...

The cops were amiable and gentle in their demeanor.

"We're not going to take him in, Sir, because your son has been so nice and polite. Just an otherwise great kid..."

With that, they produced Peter from the back of the squad car and handed him over to me, along with an expensive ticket. Wished us a good night...

Peter sat on the edge of an armchair. "I know you're not going to believe this, Dad, but this flying raccoon..."

I let him blurt on for a bit and then suggested he hit the hay. What on earth is there to further say, after our neighborhood has suffered an infestation of flying raccoons—your boy a hapless victim?

That Camry had been his sixteenth birthday present and I had loved that sleek black thing. Had owned it for many happy years before turning it over to Peter. It killed me to see the wreck of it in the impound lot when we went next day to sift through the condom wrappers and beer cans and busted cigarettes and rolling papers and wads of soiled tissues and stained clothes and Styrofoam cups and the other typical detritus of a teenage lad's interior.

Broke my heart.

Those frickin' flying raccoons have a lot to answer for…

ACCIDENTS HAPPEN 7

✳ HIT-AND-RUN AT THE CARIBOU DRIVE-THRU ✳

On an Easter Sunday, I was idling at a Caribou Coffee drive thru, waiting on my triple espresso. Crunch! I was jolted forward in my seat. A gray SUV had banged into my rear.

I slid out of my Chrysler 300, noted the sizable dent in my rear fender and signaled the SUV's driver. The fifty-something church lady rolled down her window about one third of the way.

"Let's pull over into the parking lot to exchange information," I said.

"Why? There is no damage," she replied.

"There most definitely is—look—so let's pull over."

I got my espresso and pulled into the lot.

Boom: she bolted, like a bat from the belfry...

Perhaps no insurance? But stupid really—she was risking a year in prison if we had tracked her down. Failed to catch her plates, however. And no CCTV. The lady escaped scot-free.

The sleezoid's final gift to me: $2,300 in repairs, a banged-up neck—and a simmering fury that poisoned me for some weeks to come.

❋ IT HURTS TO BE DOUBLE REAR-ENDED ❋

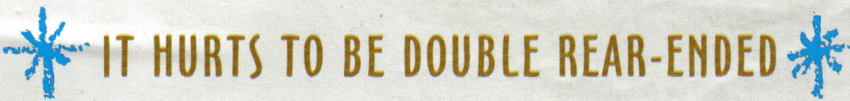

On the eve of Katrina, I'm leaving Portland Airport in a rental to attend a five-day shamanic qigong retreat on the Oregon coast with Master Wu. I'm idling at a stoplight. Before red can turn to green, the rental lurches and my head snaps back. A rust-red truck has rammed us... I turn my head to see the truck reverse away. Then, with my neck still twisted round, I watch as the truck careens forward and crashes into my rear a second time.

Let me tell you: it hurts to be rear-ended. And it hurts a hell of a lot more when your neck is twisted sideways...

The truck reverses a second time. Two minutes pass. The truck is idling, coughing up a lung... I choose to jump out and walk back to the truck. Who is this—and why me? Some kind of red-neck road rage? A wacked-out meth freak? What next, a pistol in my mouth then my brains on the sidewalk?

Turns out to be this weather-beaten old dude in a cowboy hat. He stutters a mortified apology. He's been at a cancer treatment and evidently the chemo got the best of him: he'd had lost control of his foot on the pedal. Twice. What could I say? And it was bizarre enough to believe. I wished him well and headed back to Hertz for a replacement.

The accident had an ironic consequence. Rushing to relax at the retreat on time, I floored it through the winding, pine-clad mountain roads and through the sleepy coastal towns, until I finally got nailed for speeding by a local trooper.

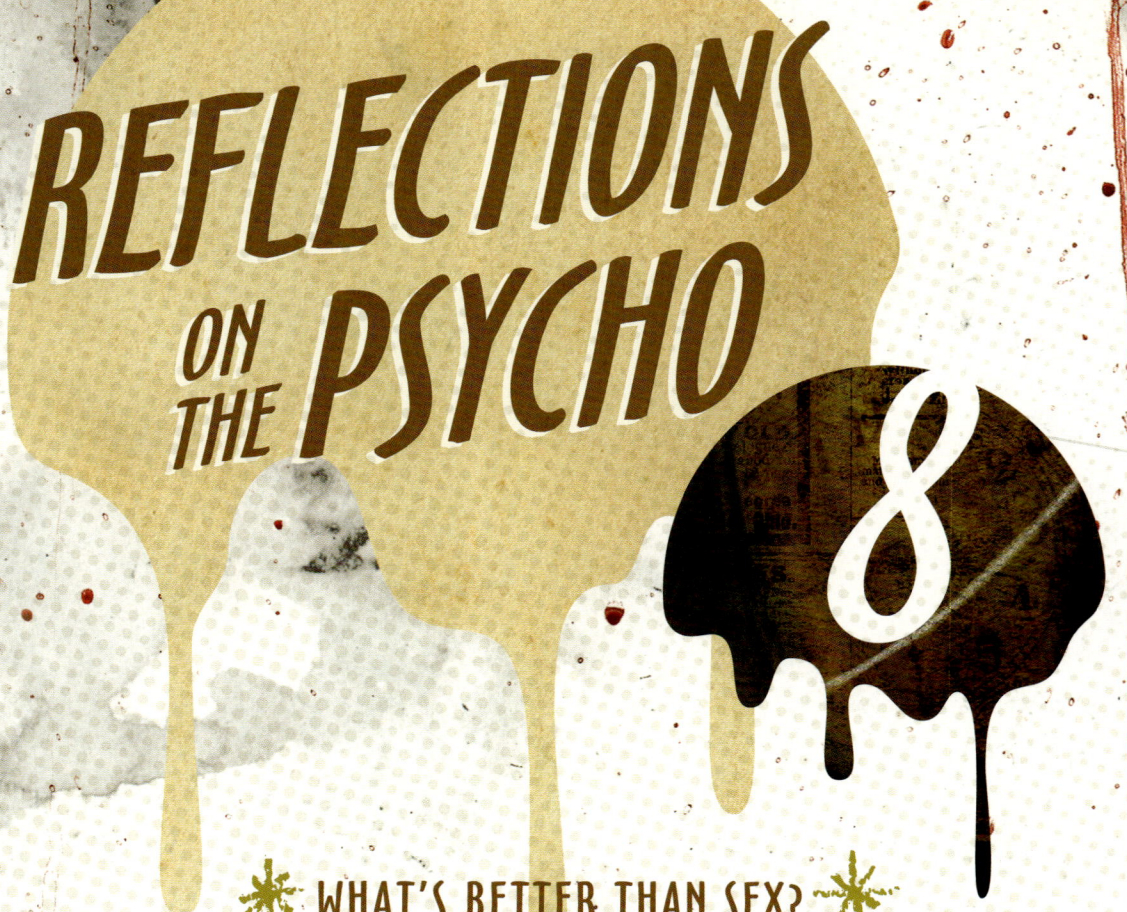

REFLECTIONS ON THE PSYCHO

8

✳ WHAT'S BETTER THAN SEX? ✳

My friend Jake, the natural-born thug, leaned his hard, shaved skull in close to my face and whispered with earnest intimacy, "I tell you John, nothing beats blowing someone away with a shotgun. Nothing. It's better than sex." He belched. Stale beer and nicotine and acrid garlic burned my nose.

And what could I say but to cover my mouth with my fingers and nod and arch my eyebrows, as if to reflect that "damn—and all this time I'd thought sex was the be-all-and-end-all?"

I've had a few folks confess murders to me over the years, but Jake was in a class of his own. The innocent pathologic, with no heart to call his own. A rolling cannonball on a pitching deck. The killer with a gleam in his eye… Yet charming and funny and good company like only the best of psychopaths know how to be…

Jake had been describing his hit on two young gals who had overplayed their hand with a local mobster. Opened up on them in their bedroom with a sawn-off double-barreled shotgun. Then chopped off their hands and heads and dumped them in a local well. The pub stool squeaked as he shifted his weight to turn and survey the vicinity. Satisfied his secret was safe with me, he gave me a twisted half-smirk then stared thoughtfully at the shadowed mirror that ran behind the bar.

Jake was built like the proverbial brick shit house—squat, thick, low to the ground. A pugilistic man—a brawler and a mauler who could fisticuff and hold his own with any comers. He was particularly adept at head-banging. Once I watched when—annoyed at a drinking buddy—he leapt out of his seat to smash his forehead onto the gentleman's nose. Broke it with a pop and a crack and a flood of blood.

I am glad to have stayed on his good side for the period I knew him…

I've seen plenty of vets and addicts break down in real tears recounting atrocities they've been party to: staving in old ladies' heads with a crow-bar when snatching their purse on a dark street for dope, beating debtors to pulp with a baseball bat, opening up on women and kids in a hooch in Nam—and so on and so on. The remorse is evident. But then there is the casual confession of a killing done "just because." More of a matter-of-fact description with not a hint of emotion. Chilling and sobering in its banality of expression. Like this other friend who told me how, oh by the way, he had once stabbed a fat Turk in an altercation in Istanbul. "He let out this weird squeaking sound, as my blade went into him. Weird. Then I pulled it out, wiped it clean and ran for it." End of story—and now, what shall we eat for dinner?

Me? I'm gonna stick with sex…

I SCREAM

Spread my legs and let my balls hang down. Arch my back. Stick my butt out. Lean forward, palms against the wall. Naked. And wait…
The blindfold itches tight on the eyelids. Fugitive whispers. The clink of ice in metal buckets. The slosh of water. Hot breath on my cheek. Silence. The padding of feet. Silence. Wait. Wait. Wait.

Then the air seems to suddenly thicken with intent. Action explodes out of the dark: a searing flick on startled buttocks from a wet towel whipped across the pink flesh. A sudden shout against the left eardrum. A burst of icy water on the back. A fingernail flick to the scrotum. Their fun had begun…

I didn't just volunteer and I wasn't shanghaied. I had paid real money. It was part of a 48-hour marathon encounter group—originally designed to get junkies in touch with their feelings. The current joy ride modeled itself on British interrogation tactics with the IRA.

The big idea was to bludgeon the defended seeker into a blubbering jelly of unrepressed emotions. A bully boy approach to driving out the demons through cathartic beat downs.

But I blew the whole deal…

Instead of letting myself be genuinely hazed into vomiting up my stiffly-held secrets, I sabotaged the process with survivalist histrionics. I screamed. I hollered. I cried. I puffed. I shook. I whimpered. I did everything to convince my tormentors I was deep into a bona fide release.

In this, I succeeded brilliantly. I fooled them. After the joyride had climaxed, the blindfolds removed and we victims were milling around in a kind of dazed stupor, the group leader proudly congratulated me on my breakthrough.

Thing is, I had felt nothing. My defenses had held. In fact, I had failed as brilliantly as I had succeeded. I had treated the method as a game to be won. But the joker was trapped in the lobster pot of his own cleverness. His loss. My loss.

In the late seventies, I invested in a Santa Claus horror movie, *Christmas Evil*, produced by my friends Bert Kleiner and Pete Kameron. Only $5,000—which, I believe, went straight up their ample noses. Naturally, I never saw a dime back. They took me, but I don't feel that badly about it. I have affectionate memories of our wild times together and the great, meandering, speedball-laced conversations.

Pete was the founder of the *L. A. Weekly* and The Who's record label Track Records—amongst a hell of a lot else. Bert was a one-time hot shot investments hustler, then producer of *The Secret Life of Plants*, Jodorowsky's *The Holy Mountain* and other outré offerings. He was a resplendent, debauched rogue of a man, in the grandest of Hollywood traditions.

Christmas Evil went on to become a much-appreciated cult classic, with John Waters leading the charge of admirers...

Around 1985, a horror buff buddy turned me on to another beauty called *Silent Night, Deadly Night*, a cult shocker about a crazed Santa serial killer. For the longest time, I thought that *this* was the film I had invested in—and would share its bizarre tale with any who'd care to listen or watch.

There's a scene in *Silent Night, Deadly Night* that made a particular impression, amongst a slew of hilarious moments:

Two young boys visit their catatonic grandfather in a nuthouse. The elder kid is left alone with grandpa—while the parents consult with the psychiatrist, younger child in tow. Grandpa's eyes suddenly crack open. His head swivels. He fixes the kid with a penetrating gaze.

"Have you been a good boy? Or have you been a naughty boy? Because, if you've been a naughty boy, Santa's going to get you..."

"NAUGHTY" BECAME ONE OF MY FAVORITE WORDS

At which point, the parents return—and grandpa's head snaps back into catatonia, eyes blank.

Shortly after, the parents stop for a hitchhiking Santa. Santa promptly pops a cap in dad then slits mom's throat after a fumbling rape attempt. The kids flee through barbed wire into the snowy forest with Santa bellowing after them, "Come back here, you little bastards!"

The "naughty" refrain gets notched up a couple of clicks at the orphanage, run by a deranged, sexaphobic Mother Superior. Then "naughty" notches up again when the older boy as a teenager is forced to be Santa at a local toy store. When he finds his love-crush in the storage room being groped by the slimy manager, Santa flips his wig and mayhem is unleashed. Santa goes on a madcap serial slashing spree which ends back at the orphanage.

The trope continues to build through to the final climax. "Naughty" is the very last word of the movie, menacing in its promise of future retribution...

"Naughty" became one of my favorite words. I wheel it out frequently—if possible accompanied by a downward twist of the mouth and a certain hardening of the eyes...

PHYSICAL FOOLISHNESS 9

✳ THE SWEET REVENGE OF GODDESS PELE ✳

Y2K. The night of the reckoning was upon us. Would the web unravel and planes fall out of the sky? Would the maddened, chaotic starving masses fan out across the countryside—fangs bared—pillaging and scavenging and rioting?

We huddled on the slopes of Kilauea. Bitter winds gusted through our skinny shirts and skirts. We stomped our sandals on the rough-cracked rock which glittered from the pale moon. We rubbed blue hands. We exhaled sharp bursts of steam from tight lips. Eyeballs glistened, brows furrowed, shoulders hunched. We struggled to relax and do what we had come to do: connect with the Big Dipper using ancient and arcane Taoist chants and hand signs special imaginings. We were hear in our own way to sanctify the New Millennium.

We finished at the tick of midnight. And as we completed, the dark lands below erupted in a relief of fireworks. Faint cheers wafted up from distant villagers.

With some regret, we let our anticipation of the Apocalypse subside... We hugged in gratitude, before hiking back down the lava-laced path. Next morning on New Year's Day, we had a date with the dolphins at the black sand beach near Kalani Honua. Would the dolphins get the invitation? And would they care?

Led by sweet-faced Grandmaster Shou-Yu Liang, we circled our arms, breathed into our bellies and sent seductive telepathies into the stolid seas.

No humps broke the surface, no smiling faces swum toward us, no creatures ventured to come play the game.

The waves picked up in a chop and threw themselves at our feet with surly disdain.

Disappointed, we milled around in a gaggle of uncertainty, before relaxing into banter and horseplay.

A thick-bodied massage therapist, Mariah, began to pick up stones from the beach and slide them into her quilt bag. Not good, as Big Island legend would tell you. The Goddess Pele is a jealous lady—and nails the fool who dares to steal her stuff.

We warned Mariah, but she would have none of it. "The stones belong to the people!"

She stuffed her bag then stepped down to wash herself off in the ocean. A wave reared up and slammed her down with an angry hiss of spray.

Mariah screamed. She'd wrenched her back. A few of us attempted to work on her, but Pele had done her job and the painful writhing persisted...

As instigator and organizer of this Qigong Millennial Retreat, I did a stupid thing, hoisting Mariah onto my back, manhandling her up the cliff side.

This didn't sit well with the Goddess. I felt a sharp stab in my own back. Steely claws clutched at my neck. Payback for aiding the pebble-thief.

I am not sure what Mariah's eventual fate was, but I was badly knotted-up for the next couple of weeks. It took the magical method of a Blair practitioner to finally release me into pain-free movement.

Pele plays it hard and long—remember that when you visit her shores...

PELE PLAYS IT HAR
AND LONG—

REMEMBER TH
WHEN YOU VI
HER SHORE

72

THE TURKISH ARMY TRUCK

Driving through Turkey in 1969 had its own set of traffic-related challenges. A round-about might as well have had signs that said: "Direction Optional" and "Make Way If You Feel Like It." Once, laboring up a steep hill near Ankara, I had to veer entirely off the road—because three battered trucks had just rolled over the brow of the hill, abreast.

But our experience with a Turkish Army troop transport near Mount Ararat took the cake…

The transport was lumbering along in the middle of the road forever and a day, making it impossible to pass. Cheerful soldiers waved at us through the rear canvas flapping in the wind.

Suddenly, the truck switched to the wrong side of the road—and stayed there.

Okay…

I gunned our pathetic excuse of a VW engine and started to overtake the truck.

Which is what they were waiting for…

We were almost past them when the driver swerved to hit us and caught our back. We careened toward the ditch, but our speed was just enough—and we fish-tailed to safety ahead of the truck.

We looked back at the driver and his mate: they were splitting their sides.

Nice set up guys…

HOW TO FINGER DEATH
WHILE WINDSURFING IN A SPEEDO

Windsurfing without a wetsuit on a windy day off the coast of Dinard, Brittany. Skinny guy, with just a Speedo between him and the elements. A chop to the ocean. A bone-chilling cold...

I am at best a poorish windsurfer, with scant skills and not much nautical sense to back it up. So, when the tides and the sudden gusts conspired to strand me far from the rocky shore, I ended up dismasting, lying on the board and paddling.

I am not sure how many shiver-shaken hours I spent out there, but long enough to be brutally chilled.

About two weeks later in Minnesota, I developed a feeling of tightness and constriction on the left side of my chest. I labored to breathe without pain. When I started to also heat up and my temperature blew past 103, I headed to urgent care.

The physician did her best to hide her alarm. Glad I couldn't read her mind...

They stuck me in the back with a massive syringe—and siphoned out a pint or so of yellow fluid. Pleural effusion, they called it.

The medical staff rescued me from the immediate crisis. However, they had no idea about what may have caused the condition—or what to do to prevent it in the future.

My acupuncturist, Chris Hafner, was entirely unsurprised. "A classic case of wind invasion!" he observed. Chris treated me with needles, herbs—advised including pork chops, mushrooms, green beans and astragalus in my diet. The protocols worked. The condition subsided and never returned. East and West had gang-tackled me back to health...

HERE, SMOKE THIS OIL

In 1973, a friend of mine smuggled hash oil back from Nepal in film cans. I got into the prolonged and persistent habit of drinking that godly goo—mixed into a cocktail with Cointreau.

Or, I would stick a cig into a bottle of the black tar and fire that up.

Or, I would soak tobacco in a hash oil solution, bake it in the oven, then roll up spliffs from the proceeds.

While the subsequent zone-out was perfect for listening to Dub Reggae or endless repetitions of *Catch a Fire*, it did zippo for my work and social life. I became increasingly isolated in my own befuddled reveries. Hovering above my body, I feared danger behind every corner.

The International Festival of Independent Avant-Garde Film in September included a party for all the film makers—a wild bunch, to put it mildly. I brought a heavily-laced Cointreau bottle to the gathering and offered free slugs to all comers. As a result, the party disintegrated into madness and mayhem...

The principal host, Annabel Nicholson, was infuriated and felt that I had destroyed the party, accusing me of a "Fascist" act.

I hosted my own party for the film makers a couple of days later. The angry and resentful stayed away out of protest— but there were plenty of hopefuls to take up the slack—and hopefully get another hit or two of that glorious cocktail.

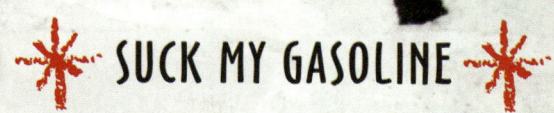

SUCK MY GASOLINE

I forget her name—and let's keep it that way. Met her around '69 in London. She was an American living in Paris. We were both broke—and somewhere and somehow, I agreed to a wild scheme of hers to defraud her insurance company.

The plot was this: we would drive from Paris to Turin, Italy. Spend the night and drive back. She would report that a bunch of her stuff was stolen from her car in Turin. We would split the final take 50/50.

There was a hitch: we had no gas money for the trip. So I agreed to syphon the gas we needed, all the way to and from.

Now, prolonged sucking of gasoline is probably not good for your health—and it also makes you high as a kite in a gale.

Case in point: It's Nice, at 2 in the morning and we find ourselves jammed between two vehicles on a side street. We bump forward and end up hooked to the front vehicle's rear fender. No worries. We accelerated backwards—and the rear fender came ripping off with an immense metallic screeching noise. We high-tailed it out of there and in our frenzy, came darn close to driving straight into the ocean.

Turin was not good to me. The lady at the cheapo hotel was outraged at the idea of the two of us un-marrieds taking a room together. I slept fitfully in the car that night, surrounded by reeking gas cans.

Our return to Paris was a grogged-out mess of a drive. How we avoided slamming into a tree or creaming a pedestrian or colliding with another vehicle remains an enduring mystery.

My final pay off for this escapade was surely the hardest-earned money I ever made.

SHIT, BUT BEAUTIFULLY COOKED

My dad was on an extended sailing trip with some mates. They shanghaied Henry into being the galley slave. The claim was that he was such a damn fine chef, it would be a crime against the profession for anybody else to be cooking up the grub.

Henry put up with this nonsense for a few days, then he flipped his lid. After retrieving the contents of his bowels, he prepared my dad and his mates a special meal. Very special...

On deck, the plates were served out. Jacques was ahead of the game and forked in a mouthful of the main dish. Jacques looked thoughtful for a moment then lent over the side and spat the half-masticated, fried turd into the unsuspecting ocean waves.

"Shit," said Jacques, "but beautifully cooked!"

This apocryphal story stayed with me into my Cambridge days and inspired me to cook a special dinner of shit burgers for two of my Eng. Lit. buddies. I fried up my shit in patties—liberally spiced with Garam Masala—then presented the carefully-garnished burgers on my best china.

My mates had done me no wrong, so fair's fair, I waited until Chris and Fred had a piece each poised at their lips before screaming "Stop!"

Being very stoned-out at the same time, they took the prank in good stride—and to the best of my knowledge there was never any pay back...

THE EXPLODING EYEBALL

In 2012, At Bill and Allison Helm's Taoist Sanctuary in San Diego, I took Chen Style Cannon Fist from Grandmaster Chen Xiaoxing. Cannon Fist is a very athletic form, with rapid, explosive strikes—and one spectacular, 360-degree "jump and pound" move. Out of a desire to burn that move in—and to impress Chen Xiaoxing with my dedication—I pounded away at that one technique with maniacal intensity and foolish frequency.

I was 63 at the time. I have some toughness, but it was senseless to put my ravaged right knee through that extended plyometric pounding. However, there was a far more significant age-related vulnerability lurking in the shadows...

When I woke up the next morning, I could barely see out of my left eye. A dirty, gray mist floated and squiggled across my retina. Was I about to go blind in one eye? Or both eyes?

I rushed to the eye specialist. "Nothing I can do for you," he said. "You have floaters. They may stay, but if you are lucky they will just subside over time."

Thanks doc!

Online research: particles of collagen and hyaluronic acid had broken loose within the eyeball—an age-related vulnerability that doesn't appreciate repetitive shocks and jolts. The good news was that the jumping and pounding hadn't resulted in a retinal tear—which could, indeed, have led to possible vision loss.

The apparent floaters remained for longer than I liked, to the point that I considered a radical laser treatment. The physician I eventually visited told me that what had really happened was some micro-bleeding within the eyeball—and that I was experiencing the visual effects of that blood swirling around. Nice. He declined to operate, telling me the condition would slowly disappear, which it did.

TRAVEL TALES

10

✳ BUGGING OUT WITH THE CRIMINALLY INSANE ✳

I don't advise getting bombed out of your mind in the number one maximum security prison for the criminally insane in the United States.

In 1970, underground filmmaker John Schofill had noted a phallic water tower he wanted to capture for his movie. He parked nearby and started prepping his Ariflex. I figured I might as well pick up a few frames myself with my 16mm Bolex.

I was clipping away at the big phallus, when a police jeep screeched to a halt next to me. "You're under arrest. You're photographing on state property." Inviting me to join them in their jeep, we headed over to pick up Mr. John and his Ari...

I noted the barbed wire and gun towers, as we were led inside the building. Electronic doors and Mengele-like men in white coats hinted at some true nasties lurking around the corner.

The guards figured we were part of some radical group like SDS, making an anti-establishment documentary. They grilled us on who we were and what we were up to.

John was not being very communicative. His eyes were bugging out of his head and he kept staring at me in a creepy kind of way. What I didn't know until later was that he was stoned out of his gourd. We had had a stash of psilocybin mushrooms in the car—and he ate all of them when he saw the police jeep approaching.

They kept us for around four hours while they checked me out with the British Embassy and checked John out with the Chicago Art Institute, where he was supposedly teaching film.

Once we checked out clean, the guards became very amiable indeed. The warden's parting, genial offer: "Hey, if you ever want to come back and make a film here, we'll see what we can do for you…"

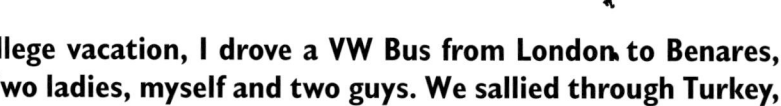

CAN I KILL YOU WITH THIS PEN?

In 1969, on a college vacation, I drove a VW Bus from London to Benares, India and back. Two ladies, myself and two guys. We sallied through Turkey, Iran, Afghanistan, Pakistan—on the hippy trail of the times…

One of my Cambridge mates on the trip, Mali Mustapha, was a Tanzanian of Pakistani origin. His uncle was a captain in the Pakistan Air Force. We stayed with the uncle in Peshawar, on the edge of the Khyber Pass.

The Captain had bombed a local tribal chief's village some time back. They'd met later at a party and became best of friends…

"I bombed your village, haha!"

"You bombed my village, I love you man, haha!"

The Chief had his own private arms factory up in the mountains. He invited the five of us to check out his village and stash of weapons.

The factory was not much more than a series of open, wooden sheds, really. But there they were, churning out rifles and pistols of every kind and make.

The Chief gave me a gift of a metal fountain pen that fired a .22 bullet when you pulled back and released its pocket clip. Smirking, he unscrewed the end of the pen, aimed at the sky—and popped a cap.

My most treasured souvenir from the whole trip...

RIFLES AT THE BORDER

The VW Bus, painted with red Sanskrit mantras, putters up to English Customs after disgorging from the ferry.

Stuffed in the back: loot from the overland trip to India. Wolf skins, Afghan jackets, Lee Enfield rifles, ancient temple artifacts, flamboyant hippie clothing, strings of big-beaded malas, rugs—oh and a bunch of hash stashed in a large calor gas container...

Hash? Now, that was not very sensible of us—as we drove that hash back with us through Afghanistan, Iran and Turkey. None of these countries were known for the niceness of their prisons.

"Anything to declare?" asked Customs Guy.

"Yes," I replied. "Two rifles."

"Two rifles!" He was confounded.

I handed the Enfields over for inspection. Supposedly they had been captured

"YOU BOMBEI

I LOVE Y

HAH

or stolen from the British Army, at some point, in Afghanistan.

Customs Guy scoffed. "No problem, these are not rifles! If they had been, we would have had to confiscate them."

Turns out, these guns were ancient enough that their barrels had no rifling. So, we were off the hook...

The officer was sufficiently thrown by the Lee Enfields, to not even ask what else we might be carrying—or to carry out any kind of search. He didn't even look at our passports to see where we had come from—or care apparently.

We all had a good laugh of relief, once safely out of his range.

 ## GO BACK TO YOUR ROOM, YOU ARE UNDER INVESTIGATION

The Shangri La Hotel, Qingdao, China, 2009. Here to visit kettlebell factories. Time for breakfast before meeting up with my Chinese contacts. 7:30am, I step out of the elevator...

Seven men in black block my way. A lady approaches at a cautious distance and tells me: "Go back to your room. You are under investigation." A calmness washes through me. Nothing like a threat of this kind to help still the chattering mind and sink me into watchfulness.

No one joins me in the elevator. "Why no escort?" I wonder.

Inside my room, I hear a rustling outside the door. Peer through the peephole. Yellow crime tape crisscrosses the corridor in front. Of my door. I retreat.

The bell buzzes. I open. Two men in Hazmat suits enter. "Relax," says one of them. His eyes smile at me.

No sweat, I am being detained by the Chinese Government for the next full week...

Turns out that a passenger on my flight from Narita has come down with Swine Flu (which they now estimate killed around 284,000 people worldwide that year). The government has tracked down every person on my flight for isolation and observation.

The smiling CDC men in the Hazmat suits fitted me out in a similar rig. My entire belongings got bagged up in heavy plastic. The CDC escorted me into the bowels of the hotel, as anxious staff peered around the corners. Then up to a large, isolated suite. A golden cage.

The mood remained light-hearted. I persuaded one of the gentlemen to photograph me in Tai Chi poses while in my Hazmat—perfect for social media...

Living in the lap of luxury at the expense of the Chinese Government was a fair trade for the loss of my freedom for a week.

I coughed one time. The phone rang. "You cough, take temperature now."

Another day, I wasn't feeling hungry and didn't eat my lunch. The phone rang. "You don't eat lunch. Why?"

They released me with kindness on the seventh day and I hooked back up with my Chinese kettlebell colleagues.

YOU VERY STRONG. WHY?

I love bodywork of all kinds. I particularly love Chinese bodywork—Tui Na, foot massage, you name it. When I am in China I get a massage every day—the price is right, the skill-level is out of sight and the experience is almost always fantastic. I leave feeling relaxed and energized.

The English language skills of the Chinese massage therapists can be quite limited—and my own Chinese a joke. Our communications become a mixture of grunts, hand signals, smiles, grimaces, laughter, groans and the occasional cryptic comment.

My favorite quote of all time was in Qingdao. After beating on me for 90 minutes, my Chinese therapist exclaimed "You very strong!" Then she paused, looked puzzled and asked: "Why?"

Being doped up on a 90-minute proprioceptive-neuro-buzz, I failed to provide a coherent answer. But the incident dramatizes the fact that you can't take your own drive for physical cultivation for granted. And for many people—even skilled bodyworkers—it's apparently a mystery that you have a strong body at all. Or why you bother...

Part of the answer lies, of course, in Michelangelo's comment "If people knew how hard I worked to gain my mastery, it wouldn't seem so wonderful at all."

The obese monstrosities waddling around Walmart didn't drop from the sky that way. They slobbed themselves into those globs of egregious fat. Those of us who choose to defy entropy—and cultivate ourselves as physical specimens—work to earn our bodies.

So: Why be strong? For hundreds of reasons, really—most of them functional. But for now, let's answer in terms of a species-basic, primal reality: body-pride and self-pride.

We are animals that are blessed with the uncanny ability to transform ourselves physically—both in function and form. Diligent work physically transforms you mentally and spiritually—while molding you into a more handsome/beautiful specimen.

You only have this one body in this life—and the older you get the more you appreciate that.

RECKLESS IN GIZA

In 1975, I bought a ticket from London to Bombay on Egypt Air, on my way to the Bhagwan Rajneesh ashram in Poona, India. We stopped for the night in Cairo...

Sleepless in my empty hotel room, I watched the full moon pouring through the broken window panes. It hit me: why not head out to the Great Pyramid of Giza nearby, climb to the top of it and meditate as the sun rose to flood me with light? A transcendental experience if ever there was one to be had...

Before dawn broke, I was out by the Great Pyramid and looking for a way to climb up. A raggedy, emaciated creature limped up to me. "You cannot climb the pyramid, it is forbidden!" He paused, "But for one pound, I show you secret way."

Up he scampered, with me in tow. We reached the top with perfect timing, just before the sun was about to rise. I crossed my legs into a full lotus, closed my eyes and readied myself for my profound mystical moment.

There was a tug on my sleeve and a hiss from my guide. "You want souvenir from Egypt?" I looked round. He was pointing at his bulging crotch. So much for my transcendental experience. I unfolded my legs and clambered back down the pyramid, pursued by his urgent pleadings.

Fortunately, a young Scandinavian lady appeared on top of a sand dune and my guide ran toward her, for his next hustle of the day. I was freed to be alone with the Great Sphinx in the still-early dawn, his chipped face and broken eyes impassively reflecting on the sexual sabotage of my spiritual moment.

PAN-FRIED WASPS ON THE HOLY MOUNTAIN

The most special meal I have eaten in my life was in the valley of a Taoist holy mountain near Qingdao, China. Mt. Laoshan was a dreamscape of phallic rocks, labial crevices, glittering streams, serene pools and wind-brushed trees. A classic painting sprung to life.

My Chinese hosts and I hiked on the magical tracks for hours of quiet ecstasy. Late in the golden afternoon, we sat satisfied at a restaurant serving specialties from the mountain. The deepest, most yellow of eggs, the richest and most succulent of greens, and mysterious mushrooms with rumored healing powers...

But the greatest delicacy was the pan-fried wasps. You just had to get over those twin demon eyes staring out at you from the plate—and the intact sting in the tail. Crunching down on those critters provoked as rich a taste-explosion in my watering mouth as I could ever have hoped for.

BORDEAUX REDS IN RIOT

In 1973, I presented a film of mine at an independent film festival in Bordeaux. My invitation had been greased by the vampire-cloaked Belgian eccentric Roland Lethem.

My film caused a riot. Punch-ups flared in the audience. Roland and I barricaded ourselves in the projection booth as furious patrons thumped on the door, wanting to tear the film off its spools. Glassy, swollen-faced, bearded types gesticulated and brandished cardboard between the light beams and the screen.

At the end of the debacle, I braved the crowd. One young gentleman in particular tossed insults in my direction. The gist was that my abstract structuralism was a form of "aristocratic elitism"—a whorish insult to the proletarian sensibility.

This was a period of leftist fervor in independent film circles—where wonky camera shots of angry workers waving fists in front of padlocked factory gates was the way to go... Agitprop.

Despite all the posturing and fist waving, nobody physically attacked me. I left the auditorium intact.

The next evening, I boarded a sleeper for Paris. The compartment door slid open and in walked my Insulter from the riot. Alone without his compadres, he looked sheepish and gave me an awkward nod.

We traveled together to Paris without exchanging a word...

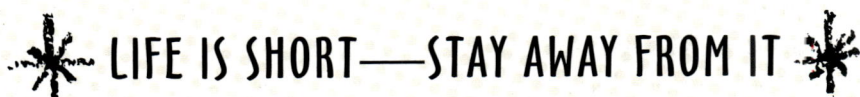

LIFE IS SHORT—STAY AWAY FROM IT

Back in the day, I was waiting inside a local Caribou to pick up my triple espresso. This frumpy, plump lady bloused into the shop and closed on the barista. She let out a sudden squawk: "Life is short, stay away from it!"

She had misread the Caribou slogan: "Life is short. Stay awake for it!"

They served her anyway...

This vignette has lodged in my mind ever since. You could riff for hours on the philosophical nuances of fleeing from life vs. engaging life full tilt.

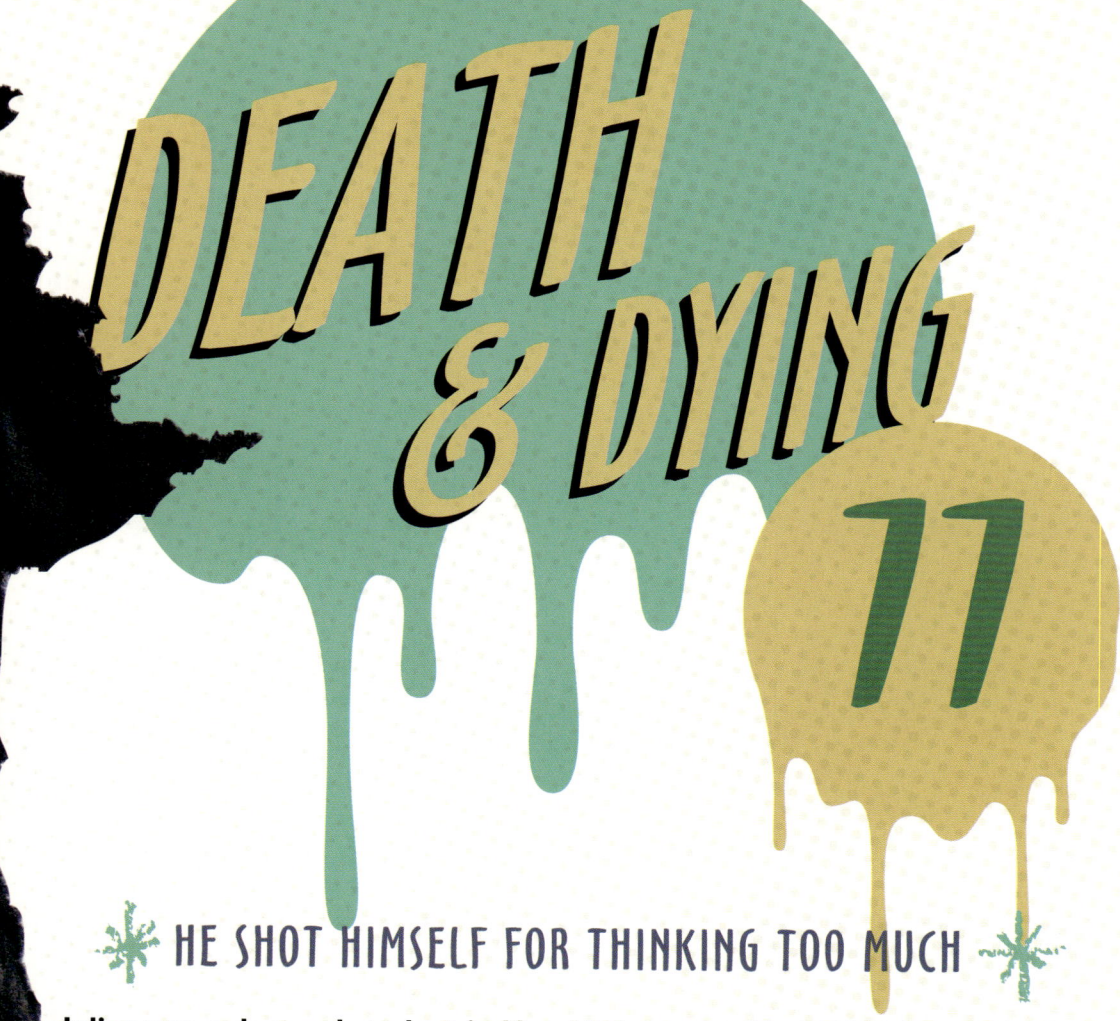

DEATH & DYING

11

✳ HE SHOT HIMSELF FOR THINKING TOO MUCH ✳

Julian was a doctoral student in Moral Sciences at Cambridge. I met him in the street one day and after some discussion invited him to take an empty room in the house I was renting. He accepted.

Julian told me later that he had been on his way to buy a shotgun to blow his brains out. He decided to give life one more chance on receiving my invitation. But it turned out to be just a temporary stay of execution...

My philosopher friend also confessed to having murdered a tramp late one night on a Cambridge commons. I had little reason to doubt the sincerity of his confession, which was delivered with barely a hint of emotion.

Julian was one tortured cat. Also, one of the most brilliant minds I've ever met. His was a terrifying inquiry into the nature and meaning of life that brooked no quarter. He sought out the greatest philosophers of his generation—in person—attempting to solve the mysteries of the universe. With not much joy.

It was impossible to hold a superficial conversation with Julian. The casual banter that lubricates relationships would devolve in a heartbeat into an agonizing analysis of some arcane puzzle with no foreseeable solution.

Julian thought himself to death. I watched his thinking process spiral him up his own ass so deep there was eventually no way to back out.

So, one day, my roommate Gautaum Tendulkar found Julian's brains splashed across the back wall and ceiling of his upstairs room. Another roommate, Roger Whitney, picked up scraps of messages by Julian, discarded carefully around the garden—a final set of hieroglyphic pleas for connection and recognition of his pain...

 ## THE DOG AND THE DOCTOR'S DAUGHTER

This one dog killed my first girlfriend—she was five and I was six...

Suzie came in screaming to her dad, the mining camp doctor, a bite wound on her arm. A stray hound had given her a nip—then skulked off into the bush, never to be found.

In Sierra Leone rabies ran rampant in the mangy curs who infested the district. No such thing as a safe dog, a nice dog.

In the fifties, it took several horse needles of vaccine into the stomach to save the victim of an attack. For small children, the effects of the injections could be traumatic, even fatal. The dad decided to wait a while, in the hope his daughter was not infected. She appeared to be ok, so he held off on the vaccine.

Several weeks later, Suzie suddenly collapsed, foaming at the mouth. Too late for help, she died in agony...

THE CASUAL BANTER
RELATIONSHIPS WOULD
BEAT INTO AN AGONIZ
SOME ARCANE PUZZL
SEEABLE SOLUTION.

HAT LUBRICATES

DEVOLVE IN A HEART-

NG ANALYSIS OF

WITH NO FORE

My parents shielded us from the details of Suzie's death. But they doubled down on their warnings about the dangers of dogs. To this day, any approaching dog puts me on initial guard.

When I finally got told the full story, it always seemed too insane to be true. How could the doctor have risked his daughter's life in such a manner? I quizzed my dad, not long before he died, about this tale. Had I heard it wrong? Had memory played tricks on me? Was I making things up?

Nope, was my dad's reply. It really did happen that way...

✳ DEATH OF THE MOTHER ✳

A few years before she did die, my mother said to me, "Don't cry for us when we die. We've had a wonderful life." Spoken with a direct certainty. I thought at the time: "I wish I could end my days with that kind of a statement, but there's no way I can wrap 'wonderful' around the turbulence of my past."

And I was to learn soon enough that the tears would flow freely—the loss all mine, tinged with the regrets of missed opportunities for connection and intimacy.

I got the news from my Dad in England that my mother was dying and to fly over right away.

I was not prepared for what I would find with her as she lay on her death bed in the hospital.

Walking through the door, I saw my mother looking about one hundred years older than when I'd seen her about a month before.

My mother opened her eyes and her face transformed into a halo of radiant joy and love—no filter, just the purity of it. I burst into a torrent of tears that didn't let up for my whole visit.

It was the most transcendent experience of my life.

Clutching her wafer-thin hand, the feeling of loss and bereavement consumed me as nothing has ever done—and ever will.

My mother's last words to me, delivered with a flood of love and the clearest, happiest, most fulfilled eyes:

"You know who to say goodbye to..."

Only in her death, did I come to love my mother in the fullness of my heart—and mourn her every day since... Only in her death.

☀ DEATH OF THE FATHER ☀

My dad died on Thursday November 1st, 2012, a few months after my mother. I missed his actual death by a couple of days, which is how I feel he wanted it...

The last weekend of my father's life, Andrea and I were in the UK for an RKC kettlebell certification. The workshop was in Bury St Edmunds and we planned to visit him briefly afterwards, before flying back to the US on the Tuesday.

That Saturday, on an errand, I ended up by error on a back road of the University of Suffolk. Ahead, I saw a smallish cylinder sticking slightly out of the ground. I figured it was some kind of traffic device that had been deactivated.

Soldier on, right? I figured I would just drive over the Thing...

As my brand-new Passat rental passed over the Thing, there was a massive explosion and the car ground to a halt.

Turns out I was the victim of an infernal British invention: the Bollard. The Thing had totaled the vehicle, wrecking the engine—which was exactly what it was designed to do. How on earth the British public accept this kind of viciousness still boggles my mind.

"Well, bollocks to you, Bollard!" I spent several hours getting rescued and towed back to Heathrow Airport, where I was given a replacement rental without—mercifully—being hit with some egregious penalty for my willful foolishness.

On the Sunday evening, we made it to my dad's apartment. He was clearly in very bad shape and not wanting to engage us long. We fed him some orange juice and promised to see him next morning, before we headed back to the States.

Monday around 11am we showed up. He was sitting up on his pillows, wearing light-gold pajamas—and greeted us with an "Oh, No!" Distressed to have any company at all. We said our goodbyes quickly.

At the doorway, I heard his last words, delivered with one raised fist: "I'm not going out on you!"

We got the call on Thursday. He had died in peace that afternoon.

And dad, you never did go out on me...

WHY I ATE MY DAD

I ate my father after he died. Here's why...

At my dad's request, my brother Peter and I met in Dinard, Brittany to pour his ashes over the ocean, where he had sailed from childhood into his late seventies.

We rented the same kind of inflatable attack-boat favored by the SEALs. Our pilot turned out to be a sun-damaged, French ex-Special Forces operative.

Unfortunately, the weather on the chosen day was dreadful. Serious white caps and a howling wind. We attempted to persist and beat out into the raging waves. It was just ridiculous... So much for the leisurely, thoughtful, soulful remembrance planned.

Plan B was to hightail it into the bay beneath the chateau where my parents had lived for a while. At least we could imagine my ghostly father staring down on us from the rocky heights, as we released his ashes back into his beloved ocean.

As my brother poured the ashes into the sea, a sudden gust blew the fine dust of my dad into my eyes—coated my face with his gray, powdery remains.

We bobbed on the wild water, first fighting, then yielding to the rising and the falling and the breaking and the pitching and the spraying...

Hunkered down in the dingy, we shared a rich Breton picnic of meats and cheeses with our Spec Ops man, then called it a day.

That evening, my brother gave me a small metal container with a half-ounce or so of the ashes, which I brought back with me to Minnesota.

I'm not sure how I arrived at the thought, but:

I decided to eat some of my father's ashes. Some kind of atavistic impulse to absorb his essence. It felt like a final, sacred homage—but somehow also very forbidden, very taboo...

I chose a Sri Lankan restaurant in Minneapolis, the Dancing Ganesha. I ordered up one of their most fiery curries. Sprinkled a little of my dad into the mix—and ate him...

The act was very special—mystical really. A way of taking his being into me in the most intimate manner possible. An act of love.

I have placed the rest of his ashes in a drawer beneath my favorite Buddha.

LOU REED

The lead guitarist, singer and principal songwriter of The Velvet Underground. After leaving the Velvets, Lou went on to record twenty solo albums including *Transformer, Berlin, New Sensations* and *New York*.

PATTI SMITH

Singer-songwriter, musician, author and poet. Notable first album: *Horses*. Acclaimed titles: *Just Kids* and *My Train*.

ANDY WARHOL

Artist, director, producer and author. Leading figure of Pop Art.

ROBERT MAPPLETHORPE

Photographer, famous for his sensitive yet direct treatment of controversial subject matter.

MICK JAGGER

Singer, songwriter, actor and film producer. Co-founder and frontman of the Rolling Stones.

BIANCA JAGGER

Human rights activist and former wife of Mick Jagger.

KEITH RICHARDS

Musician, singer and songwriter, best known as the co-founder and guitarist of the Rolling Stones.

DONALD CAMMELL

Painter, screenwriter and film director best-known for co-directing the film *Performance*.

JOHN SCHOFILL

Experimental filmmaker. Professor, School of the Art Institute of Chicago.

PENNY SLINGER

Artist and author. Co-wrote and illustrated *Sexual Secrets, The Alchemy of Ecstasy*.

SANDY DALEY

Director of *Robert Having His Nipple Pierced*.

JULIAN ALLASON

Photographer, behavioral therapist, travel writer.

ROMAN POLANSKI

Film director, producer, writer and actor. Best-known films: *Repulsion, Rosemary's Baby, Chinatown* and *The Pianist*.

SHARON TATE

Actress and model. Best-known role: *Valley of the Dolls*.

SAM ROBARDS

Actor. Best-known role: *A.I. Artificial Intelligence*.

DONOVAN

Singer, songwriter and guitarist. Developed an eclectic style that blended folk, jazz, pop, psychedelia and world music.

KENNETH ANGER

Underground experimental filmmaker, actor and author.

ANTONY BALCH

Film director, best-known for *Horror Hospital*.

SKIP MARTIN

Actor, best-known roles: *Horror Hospital* and *Masque of the Red Death*.

WILLIAM BURROUGHS

Writer. Visual artist. Best-known titles: *Junkie* and *Naked Lunch*.

BHAGWAN RAJNEESH (OSHO)

Spiritual guru and philosopher.

TAYLOR MEAD

Writer, actor, performer. Best-known roles: *Lonesome Cowboys, Midnight Cowboy, Excavating Taylor Mead*.

JACKIE CURTIS

Actor, writer, singer. Best-known roles: *Flesh* and *Trash*.

GRANDMASTER CHEN XIAOXING

Principal of the Chenjiagou Taijiquan School

COMMENTARY ON THE ILLUSTRATIONS

WHAT I WANT TO TELL YOU

The stories In Wild Boy remind me of fragments that when put together present a certain portrait of the writer. So I asked Judit Tondora to use Pablo Picasso's series of Cubist portraits as the model for the illustration. I had originally suggested that the various fragments could be from different periods in my life but she wisely pointed out that the result would be overly complicated and less compelling.

I'M GONNA BURN YOUR BUSH

My original suggestion for this was to include various machete and stick-wielding Mende tribespeople. Instead, Judit incorporated a cute photo of myself and my brother from that same period into a composition which is more striking. Judit has an extraordinary ability to render the inner spirit and feelings of the event described and this is a perfect example of her skill in that dimension.

MASTER LOU

I suggested to Judit that we concentrate on the scene where Lou Reed dies doing Tai Chi in his wife Laurie Anderson's arms. Judit came up with the idea of composing it as a stained-glass Pieta and the result is transcendent.

COBRA BLOOD AND A SHOT OF SCOTCH

Debbie Harry's manager, Tommy Manzi, recommended I check out *The Beastie Boys Book* for its supreme quality. I was particularly struck by the graphic novel illustrations and hunted down the illustrator, Judit asking her if she would illustrate my Wild Boy stories in a similar manner. Fortunately for me she loved the stories and quickly sent me a brilliant set of ideas on how to best illustrate the often very different tales. Part of her concept was to use a style that truly matched the feel of that particular story. "Cobra" most closely matches the graphic novel treatment I had originally admired in *The Beastie Boys Book*.

I WAS STRANGLED AT BIRTH

I proposed a composition much as you see here. However Judit showed her brilliance again by using a style reminiscent of certain elegant Japanese erotic painters. The result is so much more layered and resonant than what I had had in mind.

BASE COCAINE AND THE BLUE LIGHT

The composition and perspective here is what I had suggested, however Judit came up with a compelling twist: instead of having Hollywood Henry looking back at me, she composed an older, perhaps wiser version of myself contemplating my drug-fueled younger being.

JACKIE BE GOOD

This is the bravest of the illustrations and I took a risk here in suggesting to Judit that she illustrate the sexual finale. Not only did Judit totally nail the three key scenes but she handled that final scene with a kind of sexy, humorous elegance. And I love the Marlene Dietrich hints with the long cigarette holder. Very clever. I think Jackie would have appreciated it...

WHEN MY DAD TORPEDOED THE BISMARCK

I sent Judit stills from the movie *Sink The Bismarck!* plus shots of my dad as a Fleet Air Arm pilot. She chose a style of comic book illustration of warcraft particularly beloved by the French — and completely nailed the feel and detail of the story. So good!

THE ILLUSTRATED WILD BOY

WHAT'S BETTER THAN SEX?

I had originally proposed a scene where the skinhead has just blown away one of the girls who lies bloody against the sofa and he is in the process of shooting the second girl, a gloating grin on his face. Instead, Judit went with the inner evil of this maniac, in the style of Menton J. Matthews. The result is profoundly shocking and disturbing—as is the story itself.

SHIT BUT BEAUTIFULLY COOKED

I guess this story hints at the frequent times in my life that I have presented my shit to my friends pretending it to be a thing of beauty. Judit had the brilliant idea of modeling this illustration on a Fifties advertisement for milk. Mix that with the strangely biblical look of the figures and you have an extraordinarily rich and resonant painting.

I SCREAM

My idea here had been to illustrate me standing naked and blindfolded, hands against the wall, as I was being whipped and otherwise abused. Judit chose an entirely different route, going for the intensity of the catharsis that was at the heart of the "therapeutic" endeavor.

BUGGING OUT WITH THE CRIMINALLY INSANE

This one we had originally conceived of as a graphic novel piece but I like how Judit took it down to one stark noir image. And the movie camera looking like a weapon of mass destruction is a great touch!

ACKNOWLEDGEMENTS

My muse for the Wild Boy stories was Debbie Harry. Debbie, thank you for the inspiration you gave me by just being your remarkable self—and thank you for the gracious appreciation of my scribblings over the period it took to refine these various stories.

Judit Tondora's brilliant illustrations for Wild Boy blew me away—and then some. Judit, you are magnificent and I treasure our creative collaboration. Here's to many more ventures together in the future...

Speaking of brilliance, I was astounded at the creativity, imagination and skill that Ian Koviak and Alan Hebel of theBookDesigners brought to every aspect of the book's design. They immeasurably exceeded my expectations. Thank you so much guys!

Gratitude to my brother Peter Du Cane for his unswerving help in fact-checking the stories and providing me with countless photographs from our shared past.

And a thank you to Laura Phillips for her invaluable feedback, both for the stories and the final design. I will remain forever grateful for her wise counsel and strong support of the project.

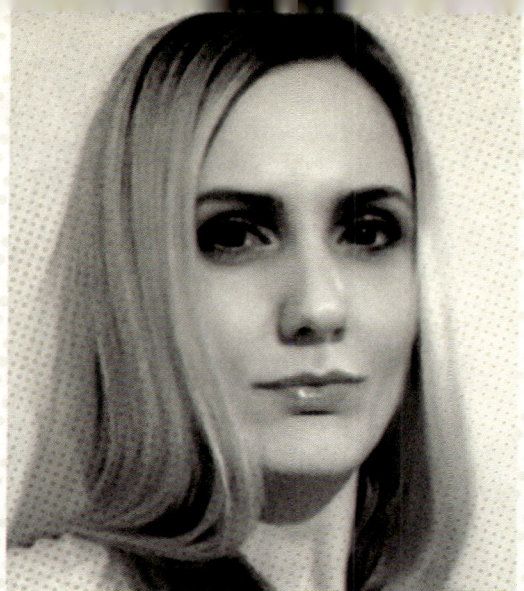

ABOUT JOHN DU CANE

John Du Cane is the founder of Dragon Door Publications, best known for having launched the modern kettlebell movement in 2001 and for publishing the international bestseller Convict Conditioning.

Educated at Cambridge University, John has had a lifelong interest in health and strength with a particular emphasis on Chinese internal martial arts and qigong. As a writer, he most recently collaborated with Debbie Harry on the writing of her New York Times Bestselling memoir, Face it.

You can reach John through his personal website: www.johnducane.com

ABOUT JUDIT TONDORA

Judit Tondora has been illustrating artworks for comics, books, games, posters, prints, magazines, trading cards, storyboards and animations for over 10 years.

Her illustrations have appeared in DC Comics and Dynamite Entertainment comics, Benchmark and Scholastic books and she has illustrated official Star Trek, Captain America, Wonder Woman and Bettie Page artworks.

Her latest licensed publication, a short graphic novel, appears in the New York Times Bestseller Beastie Boys Book.

Besides working on licensed products for Disney, additional licenses and publishers include Rittenhouse Archives, Upper Deck, CBS Studios, Marc Ecko Entertainment and Nike.

Judit runs a full-time freelance studio and can be contacted via tondoraj@gmail.com for commissioned or contracted works.